Henry David Thoreau

The light which puts out our eyes is darkness to us.
Only that day dawns to which we are awake.
There is more day to dawn.
The sun is but a morning star.

MODERN SPIRITUAL MASTERS SERIES

HENRY DAVID THOREAU

Spiritual and Prophetic Writings

Edited and with an Introduction by

TIM FLINDERS

ORBIS BOOKS
Maryknoll, New York 10545

Founded in 1970, Orbis Books endeavors to publish works that enlighten the mind, nourish the spirit, and challenge the conscience. The publishing arm of the Maryknoll Fathers and Brothers, Orbis seeks to explore the global dimensions of the Christian faith and mission, to invite dialogue with diverse cultures and religious traditions, and to serve the cause of reconciliation and peace. The books published reflect the views of their authors and do not represent the official position of the Maryknoll Society. To learn more about Maryknoll and Orbis Books, please visit our website at www.maryknollsociety.org.

Published by Orbis Books, Box 302, Maryknoll, NY 10545-0302.

Acknowledgment is gratefully extended for the right to publishing the following copyrighted publication:

Selections from Henry David Thoreau. *Journal, Volume 1: 1837–1844*. Copyright © 1981 Princeton University Press. Reprinted by permission of Princeton University Press.

Selections from Henry David Thoreau. *Journal, Volume 2: 1842–1848*. Copyright © 1984 Princeton University Press. Reprinted by permission of Princeton University Press.

Manufactured in the United States of America

Thoreau, Henry David, 1817–1862.
[Works. Selections. 2015]
Spiritual & prophetic writings / Henry David Thoreau ;
edited and with an introduction by Tim Flinders.
pages cm. (Modern spiritual masters)
Includes bibliographical references.
ISBN 978-1-62698-110-2 (pbk.)
1. Spirituality. 2. Spiritual life. 3. Transcendentalism (New England)
I. Flinders, Tim, editor. II. Title. III. Title: Spiritual and prophetic writings.
BL624.T463 2015
818′.309 - dc23 2014029313

Contents

Sources

COR *The Correspondence of Henry David Thoreau*. Edited by Walter Harding and Carl Bode. New York: New York University Press, 1958.

ESS *Essays*, Henry David Thoreau. Edited by Jeffrey S. Kramer. New Haven: Yale University Press, 2013.

JOU *The Journal of Henry David Thoreau*. Edited by Bradford Torrey. Boston: Houghton Mifflin, 1906. The journal is available online at http://www.walden.org.

LSS *Letters to a Spiritual Seeker*, Henry David Thoreau. Edited by Bradley P. Dean. New York: W. W. Norton, 2004.

PJ *The Writings of Henry David Thoreau: Journal, Volumes 1–8*. Edited by John C. Broderick et al. Princeton: Princeton University Press, 1981–2002.

WAL *Walden*, Henry David Thoreau. With an introduction and annotations by Bill McKibben. Boston: Beacon, 1997.

WCM *A Week on the Concord and Merrimack Rivers*, Henry David Thoreau. Edited by Carl F. Hovde. Princeton: Princeton University Press, 1980.

Introduction
Henry Thoreau's Profession

In March 1848, Henry Thoreau received a letter from Harrison Otis Blake, a widowed school teacher from Worcester, Massachusetts, who implored the thirty-year-old transcendentalist to correspond with him. "Speak to me in this hour as you are prompted," Blake wrote, explaining that he was determined to commit himself to a simpler and purer way of life. "But alas," he confessed, "I shiver on the brink."

The invitation was unexpected. Thoreau had yet to publish a book, while the articles and poems that appeared in small journals had left him largely unknown to a wider public. His best friend, Bronson Alcott, had remarked just a few days earlier that although he and Thoreau were valued members of Emerson's transcendentalist "club," they had failed to attract even a single "fine soul" as a disciple. Alcott wondered if they were having any effects at all in the world.

As if on cue, Blake's letter arrived. This fine soul with two young daughters had read an article of Thoreau's that prompted recollections of a conversation they had had a few years before at Emerson's house. At the time, Thoreau had mentioned his idea of retreating into the wilderness, anticipating his two-year sojourn at Walden Pond. Blake asked if he wouldn't miss the company of his family and friends. "No," Thoreau had answered, in Blake's recollection. "I am nothing,." Blake had been struck by the "poise and repose" he heard in Thoreau's remark, sensing an equanimity he found "inconceivable" in someone so young (Thoreau would have been in his mid-twenties at the time.) "If I understand rightly the significance of your life," he added, "this is it: You would sunder yourself from society, from the spell of institutions, customs, conventionalities, that you may lead a fresh, simple life with God. A new life, without and within." Though it had been some years since they last met, and then only for an afternoon's conversation, Blake was convinced that Thoreau had the depth and maturity to act as his spiritual guide. "I would know of that soul which can say, 'I am nothing,' " Blake pleaded. "I would be roused by its words to a truer and purer life."

Thoreau did not recall the conversation, but he was touched and emboldened to hear that his words had not been without effect. He welcomed the opportunity to correspond and confirmed Blake's reading of his life's intentions. "I do believe that the outward and the inward life correspond," he wrote back. "I do believe in simplicity." Thoreau cautioned Blake that since his own efforts at living a principled life gave him no occasion "to congratulate myself," his counsel would spring from his "faith and aspiration," rather than from spiritual attainment. "I am simply what I am," he confessed, remarking how easy it was for even the wisest of men to allow the trivial affairs of life to interfere with higher pursuits. Nonetheless, he wrote, there was an enduring, if faint, "glimmer of reality" that occasionally "illuminated the darkness of daylight" and was well worth the effort to experience it. "So simplify the problem of life, distinguish between the necessary and the real," he advised. "Let nothing come between you and the light."[1]

Blake's letter initiated a correspondence that would continue until the final year of Thoreau's life. In the several dozen letters Thoreau wrote Blake during the next thirteen years, he expressed his deepest spiritual longings and concerns in far more forthright and transparent language than he would bring to his articles and books. Thoreau did not intend these letters to be published—though he was aware that Blake shared them with a small circle of friends—and, in any event, believed that authentic religious feeling was beyond the scope of language. ("What is religion? That which is never spoken.") Blake and Thoreau became friends, visiting each other over the years and sharing their common struggle to find balance between the claims of the world—"getting a living"—and their higher pursuits.

As their friendship deepened, Thoreau's letters to Blake became more searching and spiritually substantive, always pressing him forward on "the journey." His first letter closes with an appeal that, typically, urges Blake onward, and that can stand—as will become clearer when we look more closely at his life—as a distillation of the singular passion that animates his life and work: "When you knock, ask to see God—none of the servants."

BEGOTTEN BY THE BREEZES 1817–1838

Henry David Thoreau was born on July 12, 1817, in Concord, Massachusetts—"the most estimable place in all the world," he would write, "and in the very nick of time, too." The third of four children, he was a quiet, studious boy with a gift for languages—he studied Greek, Latin, and French at the Concord Academy— and with a demeanor so solemn that his classmates called him "the judge." But he came alive in the natural world outside the classroom, exploring the woods and wetlands around Concord every afternoon with his younger brother and soulmate, John. Thoreau's was a close family—he often helped out in his father's pencil-making business, and he would live in the family home for most of his life.

Thoreau entered Harvard in 1834 and continued his study of languages, adding Italian, German, and Spanish to his repertoire. To help with his tuition, he taught for a semester with Orestes Bronson, a member of the New England transcendentalists and a charismatic social radical. They spent long hours at night discussing philosophy, literature, religion, and social reform. The time with Bronson proved a transformative experience, radicalizing Thoreau's worldview and ushering him into what he called "the morning of a new life." The next year Thoreau read Emerson's groundbreaking transcendentalist study *Nature,* and was smitten by his call for personal freedom and for living in accord with the inner voice of conscience: radical views in a New England culture saturated with an authoritarian Calvinist ideology. By the time Thoreau graduated from Harvard in 1837, he had embraced Emerson's philosophy and was more than ready to articulate it when given the opportunity. "Let men, true to their natures, cultivate the moral affections, lead manly and independent lives," he declared in a graduation address at his commencement exercises. "Let them make riches the means, and not the end, of existence," he said, adding, in a remarkably prescient expression of the modern environmental ethic: "The sea will not stagnate, the earth will be as green as ever, and the air as pure." He was twenty.

The Panic of 1837, America's first major economic crisis, saw banks collapse, businesses fail, and thousands of laborers thrown out of work. Thoreau struggled for months in a challenging economic climate to find a teaching position and, when he did, resigned it after a week because he refused to use physical punishment to discipline his students. After manufacturing pencils for a while for his father, he started his own school in the family home. The school thrived, and Thoreau asked his brother, John, to join him as a teacher. They moved onto the campus of their former academy, offering a surprisingly innovative curriculum that emphasized learning by doing and included ample time for hikes and boating trips. Students who could not afford the tuition attended free, and no physical punishment was used. The school flourished for three years until John's failing health forced them to close.

It was during this same period that Thoreau developed a relationship with Ralph Waldo Emerson, who lived in Concord and was regarded as one of the leading writers and intellectuals of the time. Emerson saw Thoreau as a promising writer, a young transcendentalist with as "free" a mind as he had encountered. He welcomed Thoreau into his circle and introduced him to the major literary figures of the day, who visited Emerson at his Concord home. Emerson published Thoreau's early poems and articles in his transcendentalist publication *The Dial* and shaped Thoreau's developing understanding of himself as a thinker and writer. In time, their relationship would undergo strain, especially as Thoreau's literary powers matured while Emerson's declined with age. But they remained lifelong friends.

It was most likely Emerson who suggested that Thoreau keep a journal, a decision that would contribute significantly to his ultimate reputation as a writer, social critic, and naturalist. Thoreau began the journal during the summer of his graduation and made frequent entries in it until a few months before his death, totaling more than two million words. Over the years, the journal would serve multiple functions for Thoreau as a record of his thoughts and impressions, especially of the natural world; as an exercise book where he developed material for his lectures, articles, and books; and as a richly detailed log of his empirical observations of the plants and animals he encountered in his daily walks.

But from the beginning, Thoreau understood his journal writing as essentially a contemplative practice, a record of "the ebbs and flows" of his soul and a sacramental offering to the "superior powers" that inhabit the universe. "My journal is that of me which would else spill over and run to waste," he wrote in 1841. "I must not live for it, but in it for the gods. They are my correspondent, to whom daily I send off this sheet postpaid." Undertaken with solemnity, as an act of "obedience to conscience," his journal writing functioned as a form of inverted *lectio divina*, a sacred encounter with the written word in which, having emptied himself of "every particle of will," he listened attentively to the inner voice of conscience. "If we can listen, we shall hear," he wrote, describing his practice. "By reverently listening to the inner voice, we may reinstate ourselves on the pinnacle of humanity."

And there were the ecstasies—those moments of rapturous spiritual transport that sometimes visited him when he became absorbed in the woods or along the waterways around Concord. As a teenager, Thoreau built himself a small boat in which he would lie down and close his eyes, allowing the breezes to carry him, often in a reverie, across the surface of Walden Pond. "Drifting in a sultry day on the sluggish waters of the pond," he wrote in his journal at the age of twenty-two, "I almost cease to live and begin to be . . . I am never so prone to lose my identity. I am dissolved in the haze."

These rapturous episodes—he called them "ekstasies" from the Greek, *ekstasis*, to be or stand outside oneself—appear to have been common, at least during his youth. How they occurred remained a mystery to him; they simply appeared, "begotten of the breezes," freeing him from the bonds of his physical self. "It, as it were, takes me out of my body and gives me the freedom of all bodies and all nature" he wrote in his journal. "I leave my body in a trance and accompany the zephyr and the fragrance." Along with his sense of self, time and space dissolved as well. "If with closed ears and eyes I consult consciousness for a moment," he wrote in an early attempt to describe his experiences, "immediately are all walls and barriers dissipated." He was often drawn out of himself entirely, rapt in reverie, "eternity and space gambolling familiarly through my depths . . . knowing no end, no aim." Accompanying the dissolution of self, time, and space was the presence of an abiding and ineffable peace, "the calmness of the lake when there is not a breath of wind," he wrote in his journal, "and without an effort our depths are revealed to ourselves." And in the midst of this otherworldly serenity he would find himself bathed in an interior effulgence, in which, he wrote, "I dissolve all lesser lights in my own intenser and steadier light."

While Thoreau never understood the origins of his ecstasies, observing them only from a distance "as a witness on the stand," he was nonetheless convinced of their sacred character. "I perceive that I am dealt with by superior powers," he wrote in his journal in 1851. "I feel my maker blessing me." He knew that they were gifts, and that, for unknown reasons, he had been chosen as a beneficiary. "Sometimes when I compare myself with other men, methinks I am favored by the gods," he wrote during his retreat at Walden Pond. "They seem to whisper joy to me beyond my deserts." Yet he had no explanation for how such transcendence could find its way into his consciousness. "With all your science," he asked rhetorically, "can you tell how it is, and whence it is, that light comes into the soul?"

With his grounding in a secular, Enlightenment worldview, coupled with a sharp aversion to the religious cultures of his time, Thoreau lacked a context of sacred wisdom that might have shed light on the nature of his ecstasies. As it was, he felt exceptional and alone: "I wondered if a mortal had ever known what I knew," he wrote in 1851, reflecting on his earlier raptures. He had turned to Western writers for some recognition of a "kindred" experience but, he declared, "I found none." Had the sacred traditions of medieval Catholicism not been sealed off from him by the sectarianism and prejudices of nineteenth-century Christian churches, he might have found his way to these vibrant contemplative traditions and the kindred souls who peopled them. The descriptions he leaves us of his ecstasies—with their "intenser and steadier light," breathless calm, dissolution of self, and the expansion beyond space and time—carry familiar echoes of some of the most canonical expressions of transcendent experience in the Christian tradition. Saint Augustine, for instance, describes in his *Confessions* transcendent raptures infused with calm, when "all the fantasies that appear in dreams and imagination cease, and the mind stops thinking about itself and goes quite still." Teresa of Avila wrote rapturously of her experience of a "light without a night," while the fourteenth-century German mystic Meister Eckhart describes "a light which is uncreated and uncreatable" as well as a "place in the soul which neither space nor time touches."

Recent biographers of Thoreau have noted these similarities, even locating correspondences between his more ineffable experiences and Evelyn Underhill's classical hierarchy of contemplative states. Others, noting Thoreau's lack of Christocentric devotion and the absence of religious imagery in his ecstatic encounters with an "invisible presence," place him within the apophatic tradition of a featureless divine first articulated by Dionysius the Aeropagite in the sixth century.[2] Yet these comparisons have to be weighed against Thoreau's emphatic rejection of Christian redemptive theology as observed by even the most luminous Christian contemplatives. "God prefers that you approach him thoughtful, not penitent," he wrote in 1850, "though you are the chief of sinners."

Thoreau's raptures formed the central fact of his spirituality and would shape his understanding of life and his role as a transcendentalist thinker and writer.[3] However we may regard Thoreau—as a literary stylist of the first rank, a penetrating social critic, a skilled and intuitive naturalist, a philosopher—he is, at heart, and in his own understanding, a spiritual seeker: "My profession is to be always on the alert to find God in nature," he wrote at the age of thirty-four, "to know his lurking-places, to attend all the oratorios, the operas, in nature." There could be no higher calling, no more meaningful pursuit than to attempt to pry out of nature her most sacred secrets. "If by watching all day and all night I may detect some trace of the ineffable," he asked, "then will it not be worth the while to watch? Watch and pray without ceasing. . . ."

A FAINT AND DISTANT MUSIC 1839–1845

On Saturday, August 31, 1839, Henry and John started down the Concord River on a ten-day boating excursion to Concord, New Hampshire. They had built their fifteen-foot dory themselves, fitting it with oars, masts, sails, and a pair of detachable wheels for portaging the boat around waterfalls. The brothers took their time, exploring the countryside along the way for Indian artifacts, while camping at night in the copses and meadows that fringed the river. On Monday they reached the confluence of the Merrimack River and turned to follow it into New Hampshire. That night, awake in their tent, Henry fell under the spell of a distant drumming—probably a young army recruit practicing his drills. Always acutely responsive to sound ("I thank God for sound"), Thoreau became enraptured by the rhythmic drumbeat and found himself transported. "I see, smell, taste, hear, feel, that everlasting Something to which we are allied," he wrote about the experience the next morning, "at once our maker, our abode, our destiny, our very Selves." The brothers reached Concord, New Hampshire, by the end of the week, then returned home by the same route, occasionally accepting a tow from one of the barges that plied between the New England manufacturing centers and Boston.

The next year, John and Henry both fell in love with the same woman, seventeen-year-old Ellen Sewall, who had visited Concord during the summer. John proposed marriage and was accepted, then rejected when her conservative father objected to the engagement because of the Thoreaus' radical transcendentalism. When Henry proposed sometime later, Miss Sewell, who was genuinely attracted to him, felt compelled to decline his proposal. Henry would remain single for the remainder of his life and acknowledged to his sister Sophia, shortly before his death in 1862, that he had always loved Ellen.

In 1841, Emerson invited Thoreau to live in his household, tutor his children, and serve as a handyman. He hoped that by freeing Thoreau from the responsibility of supporting himself, his literary talent could flower. Thoreau became fond of the children, especially young Waldo Emerson, and developed an enduring relationship with Emerson's wife, Lydian.[4] At the same time, Thoreau became intimate with Emerson's circle and joined in the meetings of the "transcendentalist club," which met to discuss the leading issues of the day. For transcendentalists, the highest authority was not scripture or religious doctrine but individual conscience. And while most transcendentalists were content to talk and write about this ideal, Thoreau was determined to live it. When the First Parish Church of Concord assessed Thoreau with a tax in 1840, the twenty-three-year-old refused to pay it under the threat of jail. (Someone, probably an aunt, anonymously paid the tax to avoid scandal.) Thoreau then filed a document with the town council that he hoped would insulate him from further arbitrary taxation: "Know all men by these presents, that I, Henry Thoreau, do not wish to be regarded as a member of any incorporated society which I have not joined."

For transcendentalists, the natural world was a sacred scripture as revelatory of the divine as the Bible. Thoreau certainly shared this belief, but unlike most transcendentalists, including Emerson, he was not a pantheist. Nature was "the face of God," the winds and tides the "circulations" of the Divine. But it was not identical to God. "If Nature is our mother, is not God much more?" he asked in his journal. "The red-bird which is the last of nature is but the first of God." Moreover, the natural world also revealed sacred depths within the human personality, a "rich and fertile mystery" that embraced all living things. "This earth which is spread out like a map around me," he observed, "is but the lining of my inmost soul exposed."

It may be that the most significant advantage of living in Emerson's home was the access it gave Thoreau to his library, especially to Emerson's collection of Oriental philosophy, the largest of its kind in America. Thoreau quickly found his way to some of the foundational Indian contemplative texts, reading them in French when English translations were not available.[5] What struck him most forcibly was their emphasis on interiority and their call for a contemplative detachment from the material world, a refreshing departure for Thoreau from the unrepentant materialism he found in nineteenth-century Protestant Christianity. "The Hindus are more serenely and thoughtfully religious than the Hebrews," he wrote in his journal at the time. "The [Indian] religious books describe the first inquisitive and contemplative access to God." Thoreau felt reassured by their high regard for the austere, contemplative lifestyle he prized so highly.

Even more reassuring was their understanding of the sacred character of ecstatic states like Thoreau's, which, while transcendent, lacked devotional or religious content. "I looked in books for some recognition of a kindred experience," he wrote later, "but, strange to say, I found none. Indeed, I was slow to discover that other men had had this experience." Now he recognized himself in ancient Indian texts like *The Laws of Manu* (ca. fifth century BCE), where it describes the Indian yogi (seer) as one whose mind becomes so "subdued" in meditation that "he delights in his own soul" and "by the assistance of the Spirit, he beholdeth the soul." Such passages mirrored his own rapturous experiences when, having become like "a still lake of purest crystal," he found that his depths "are revealed." The notable lack of religious imagery in their descriptions of these states corresponded as well to his own featureless epiphanies, and the recognition may have prompted his often quoted remark to Harrison Blake in a letter, "To some extent and at rare intervals, even I am a yogi."

On New Year's Day 1842, John Thoreau cut himself while shaving. He dressed the wound, then gave it no thought until a few days later when it developed a tetanus infection that progressed quickly to trismus (lockjaw). He became weak and feverish, and Henry nursed him for several days as he alternated between episodes of delirium and periods of calm. "The cup that my Father gives me," John remarked to the doctor in a lucid moment when informed that his condition was fatal, "shall I not drink it?" He said his farewells on January 11, and at two o'clock in the afternoon died in Henry's arms. A few days after John's death, six-year-old Waldo Emerson, Henry's favorite, died of scarlet fever. The losses sent Thoreau into a depression in which he stopped speaking and sat for long hours by himself. He lost interest in nature, and would not accompany his mother and sisters with his flute when they sang in the evening, one of his favorite pastimes. He developed a fever, and when he began to display the sympathetic symptoms of lockjaw, though he had no infection, his family despaired. But he eventually recovered, after being bedridden and housebound for several weeks. For years Thoreau would suffer nightmares on the anniversary of John's death and have to fight tears at the mention of his name.

But even as he struggled with his own depression, Thoreau displayed a remarkably detached view of death, accepting it as one dimension of the creation process. "Only nature has a right to grieve perpetually," he wrote to Emerson's sister in March, two months after John's death. "Soon the ice will melt, and the blackbirds sing along the river which he (John) frequented, as pleasantly as ever. The same everlasting serenity will appear in the face of God, and we will not be sorrowful if he is not." A few days later Thoreau wrote a letter of consolation to Emerson for the loss of young Waldo, suggesting that death is as common as life and even "beautiful" when seen as a function of the natural creation cycle. "Every blade in the field—every leaf in the forest—lays down its life in its season as beautifully as it was taken up," he wrote. "Dead trees—sere leaves—dried grass and herbs—are not these a good part of our life?"

In July, Nathaniel Hawthorne moved to Concord with his new bride and quickly became friends with Thoreau, who built him a small boat and taught him how to sail. In the winter, they skated together, along with Emerson, down the Concord River. Twenty-five years old, Thoreau had recovered from his depression but was feeling anxious about his literary prospects. Apart from occasional articles published in *The Dial,* his writing career had failed to materialize. In May 1843, he accepted a position as tutor to the children of Emerson's brother William, a judge on Staten Island. Thoreau hoped to use his proximity to New York City to gain entry into its publishing world, but the literary scene was already crowded with established writers, and he failed to interest a publisher in his work. However, Horace Greeley, the influential editor of the *New York Tribune*, admired Thoreau and would eventually serve him as an informal literary agent, finding placements for several of his essays.

But Thoreau found New York City uncongenial and spent most of his leisure time walking the secluded beaches and countryside of Staten Island. At the end of the year, he moved back to Concord and joined his father in the family's pencil-making business. He had a talent for mechanical invention and spent several weeks redesigning the manufacturing process his father used. Unfortunately, he told Emerson, he could do only one thing at a time, and if he made pencils during the day, he could not help making them at night when he should be writing. In any event, his innovations were so successful that his father gained the reputation for making the best pencils in the country, equal to those imported from Europe.

Thoreau continued to publish articles in *The Dial* and briefly served as its editor until Emerson discontinued the journal in 1844 because of poor circulation. The next year, wanting to eulogize his brother John, he decided to write a book about their 1839 journey down the Concord and Merrimac rivers. Feeling the need for more privacy (he was living in the Thoreau home at the time), and still wanting to experiment with a simpler lifestyle, he accepted Emerson's offer of a small plot of land at Walden Pond, where he built himself a cabin near the shore. On the fourth of July 1845, Henry Thoreau moved to Walden in arguably the most celebrated retirement from civil life since the third century, when Saint Anthony, the "father of Christian monasticism," renounced his possessions and slipped into the Egyptian desert to seek God.

But Thoreau was no anchorite—he hadn't moved to Walden to experience the hermetic way, but as an exercise in simplicity. He built his own cabin for a few dollars, and supported himself by working occasionally as a handyman while growing a cash crop of beans. "I went to the woods because I wished to live deliberately," he wrote in *Walden*, "to front only the essential facts of life." In fact, despite a reputation as a solitary, Thoreau enjoyed company as long as it did not intrude upon his writing and contemplation. His cabin was less than two miles from Concord, and he often visited his family there for meals. Visitors dropped by, invited or otherwise, and he sometimes hosted picnics. "I am naturally no hermit," he wrote in *Walden*. "I think that I love society as much as most." Children visited as well, Thoreau leading them on nature walks around the pond with the caution that "no mother bird would lose her eggs."

He used his time well, writing through the morning and producing first drafts of the two books that he would publish in his lifetime, *A Week on the Concord and Merrimack Rivers*, and *Walden*. In the afternoons, he took long, meditative walks, read, entertained guests, and observed the pond through its seasonal changes, even measuring its depths one summer, putting to rest the local legend that it was bottomless.

FREE IN THIS WORLD 1846–1850

Thoreau's second year at Walden found him spending more time away from his cabin. He visited Concord regularly, took extensive walks through the countryside, and spent several weeks in Maine. During June, he returned to his study of the Indian scriptures, finding both comfort and instruction in their careful elaboration of the contemplative life. "In the morning I bathe my intellect in the cosmogonal philosophy of the *Bhagavad Gita*," he wrote in *Walden*, "in comparison with which our modern world and its literature seem puny and trivial." He was particularly drawn to the *Gita*'s emphasis upon detached work, having agonized for years over finding an occupation that would not compromise or dilute the intensity of his spiritual life. "The struggle in me is between a lover of contemplation and a lover of action," he wrote that spring in his journal, "the life of a philosopher and of a hero . . . but the practical hinders and unfits me for the former." The first chapter of Walden, "Economy," is sharply critical of those who spend themselves accumulating unnecessary material possessions, and losing, in the process, "the better part of the man." "How shall we earn our bread is a grave question," he would write to Harrison Blake, yet he had been unable to find any guidance on the matter from Western writers. "There is little or nothing to be remembered written on the subject of getting an honest living," he wrote in his journal. "Neither the New Testament nor Poor Richard speaks to our condition."

In the *Gita*, Thoreau found a resolution to the problem that appeared to reconcile the inherent conflicts between the active and contemplative lives. Work that was undertaken without attachment to its rewards, according to the *Gita*, was not an obstacle to spiritual growth. In fact, such action was purifying. "Wise men call him a *Pandeet* [sage]," Thoreau quoted approvingly, "whose every undertaking is free from the idea of desire, and whose actions are consumed by the fire of wisdom." In this way, work could assume a sacramental quality, sanctifying the most quotidian activities. In such detached work, Thoreau wrote, citing the *Gita*, "God is the offering . . . to be obtained by him who maketh God alone the object of His works." The key to working in the world without compromising higher pursuits was the frame of mind with which work is performed. "Forsake the fruit of action," he concluded, again referencing the *Gita*, "obtain infinite happiness."

In moving to Walden, Thoreau had hoped to discover how far he could simplify his life in order "to transact some private business with the fewest obstacles." He kept meticulous records of his income and expenses, detailing them in the opening chapter of *Walden*, and concluded that he maintained himself for the two years he lived there by working just six weeks a year. His "experiment" in the simple life had proved a success, establishing a template for supporting himself that he would follow for the rest of his life. After he left Walden, Thoreau trained himself as a surveyor, an occupation that allowed him to limit the amount of time he worked, while keeping him out in the open. It helped, of course, that he had no family to support and lived in others' homes. But he always lived frugally, and took a special delight in his pared-down lifestyle. "My greatest skill," he wrote near the end of the first chapter in *Walden*, "has been to want but little."

While Thoreau was reading the *Gita* at Walden, a detachment of two thousand soldiers of the United States Army entered Mexico in "reprisals" for attacks by Mexican troops in Texas. Thoreau was adamantly opposed to what he considered an imperialist adventure and famously refused to pay his poll tax. In July 1845, he was arrested and spent the night in jail, having been released when someone, most likely an aunt hoping to avoid scandal, paid his bail.[6] "I have paid no poll tax for six years," he would proclaim in lectures. "I was put into a jail once on this account for one night" but felt that the walls seemed a waste of stone and mortar since they could not imprison his mind. As a consequence, he wrote that he lost all remaining respect for the state. It was not his first venture into political resistance, as he had been active in the Underground Railroad for some time and had harbored an escaped slave overnight in his cabin at Walden before helping him to escape to Canada. His mother and sister, Sophia, formed the "Concord Women's Antislavery Society," and Thoreau invited them to host their first meeting at his cabin.

Thoreau left Walden in September 1847, having lived there for more than two years, writing at the time that his reason for leaving was that he had "more lives to live" and could not spare more time for that particular life. Later, he would acknowledge that, in fact, he did not know why he had left Walden. "Perhaps I wanted a change," he speculated. "Perhaps if I lived there much longer I might live there forever."

It had been a fruitful two years. Along with the drafts for his two books, he had formed the beginnings of a lecture on civil disobedience that would evolve into his most celebrated essay. Thoreau had also established a daily routine of contemplative activities that would become the touchstones for his spiritual life. His days now pivoted around a quasi-monastic routine of reading and writing in the mornings and evenings and, except when he was surveying or traveling, long, meditative walks in the afternoon, often for four hours or more where he would find himself, even on the bleakest of days, "grandly related" to the sacred creation he found inhabiting the Concord woodlands. "You think that I am impoverishing myself by withdrawing from men," he wrote in his journal, rhetorically addressing the townspeople who found his daily rambles eccentric, "but in my solitude I have woven for myself a silken web or chrysalis, and, nymph-like, shall ere long burst forth a more perfect creature, fitted for a higher society." Apart from his closest friend, Ellery Channing, who Thoreau occasionally allowed to join him, or the children he sometimes led through the woods on explorations, he generally refused requests of friends to join him. "They do not consider that the wood-path and the boat are my studio," he wrote near the end of his life, "where I maintain a sacred solitude." Though

Thoreau remained irreligious in his disposition, his routine unintentionally mirrored those of a vowed Catholic monastic—the seclusion sought by a Trappist monk in his cloister, Thoreau found on the footpath that wound through Baker's Woods or along the pebbled shore of Fair Haven Pond.

In 1847, Thoreau moved back into Emerson's home while Emerson traveled through Europe on a speaking tour. Thoreau's relationship with Lydian Emerson and her children deepened, but when Emerson returned Thoreau moved into his family's home. The next year he published an account of his Maine travels in the *New York Tribune*, an essay that Emerson said was the best American writing he had read in the past decade. Thoreau's surveying work prospered as well, though he was careful to work only when he needed to.

But he wanted to establish himself as a professional lecturer, following Emerson's lead, and accepted an invitation from Nathaniel Hawthorne to speak in Salem in November. The lecture he gave was based on his years at Walden Pond and would become the basis for the first chapter in *Walden.* But Thoreau was a better writer than speaker, often reading verbatim from his notes, while forgetting to look up at his audience. He rarely received more than two or three invitations to lecture in a year, and in some years, according to a journal note from 1857, "none at all." In that same entry, he congratulated himself on being permitted to stay at home where he could spend his time more profitably than trying to entertain an unappreciative audience. "I feel that the public demand an average man—average thoughts and manners," he wrote, "not originality, not even absolute excellence." And he was temperamentally incapable of catering to his audiences' tastes, taking offense when they complained that his transcendentalist views were sometimes unintelligible. "If you wish to know how I think," he wrote in his journal with some pique, "you must endeavor to put yourself in my place."

Although his lecturing career failed to materialize, the lectures themselves proved invaluable in developing the source material for his essays as well as for some of the chapters in *Walden.* His influential essay on civil disobedience began as a lecture at the Concord Lyceum in 1847, "The Rights and Duties of the Individual in Relation to Government." Thoreau had been asked by friends why he had chosen to spend the night in jail in 1846, and the lecture is presented as an answer to their questions. Published in a small journal in 1848 as "Resistance to Civil Government," the essay elaborates upon his transcendentalist belief that there is a higher law, grounded in conscience, that takes precedence over civil law. Such was the case with the issue of slavery, Thoreau argued, and asked rhetorically, "How does it become a man to behave toward this American government," when a sixth of its population were slaves. "I think that it is not too soon for honest men to rebel," he argued, adding that if the time came when the government required Northerners to return escaped slaves to their owners, then conscience required them to break the law: "Let your life be a counter friction to stop the machine." The essay became a rallying cry for the emerging abolitionist movement, and in 1866, following Thoreau's death, it was published as "Civil Disobedience." A half century later, Mohandas Gandhi found inspiration in the essay for his nonviolent resistance campaigns against British imperialism, and some decades later it would become a touchstone for Martin Luther King Jr.'s civil rights movement.

In 1849, *A Week on the Concord and Merrimack Rivers* was published after Thoreau agreed to cover the costs of its publication. Organized into seven chapters each representing a day of the week, the book was a hybrid of travel narrative alternating with social, cultural, and philosophic observations on a wide range of subjects, many of which had little or nothing to do with the excursion itself. Reviewers found the book too digressive, and many readers, including his relatives, were scandalized by his comparison of the Buddha with Jesus—"I know that some will have hard thoughts of me," Thoreau wrote in the "Sunday" section, "when they hear their Christ named beside my Buddha." Equally offensive was his sometimes scathing critique of institutionalized religion. "It seems to me that the god that is commonly worshipped in civilized countries is not at all divine," he wrote. "Men reverence one another, not yet God." Even some transcendentalists like George Ripley, a founder of Brooke Farm, found Thoreau's remarks on Christianity offensive "to good sense and good taste." Thoreau's criticisms of the mainstream denominations of the time were aimed at their often slavish acceptance of unexamined doctrine, as well as the sectarian bigotry, driven by "puerile distinctions" that defined nineteenth-century religious cultures. "I pray to be delivered from narrowness, partiality, exaggeration, bigotry," he wrote in his journal. "To the philosopher, all sects, all nations are alike."

Although largely disaffected from the prevailing Calvinist culture, Thoreau remained steeped in its scriptural tradition, drawing regularly upon biblical allusions in his lectures, essays, and books. There are several hundred references drawn from the Bible in his journals, although he was adamantly averse to biblical doctrine, especially its eschatological insistence on a heavenly reunion with the divine reserved for the pious believer. If God were to be found at all, Thoreau reasoned, it would not be after death, but here and now and most probably in nature. "God himself culminates in the present moment," he wrote in *Walden*, and was apprehended "only by the perpetual instilling and drenching of the reality that surrounds us." The Divine dwelt within, rather than in an extraterrestrial paradise, and could be found only there. "Heaven is the inmost place," he wrote emphatically in his journal. "What sacred place can there be but the innermost part of my own being?"

A Week on the Concord and Merrimack Rivers failed to find enough of an audience to recover its publication costs, which Thoreau had guaranteed. When his publishers delivered seven hundred unsold copies to his home, he stored them in the attic and famously remarked that he now had a personal library of more than nine hundred volumes "over seven hundred of which I wrote myself." Despite the self-deprecating humor, Thoreau felt burdened by the debt and took several years, and more surveying work than he would have preferred, to reimburse his publishers.

With the growing success of their pencil-making business, largely due to Thoreau's redesigns, his family built a substantial new home on Main Street in Concord, and in August 1850, Thoreau moved into the attic, where he would live for the rest of his life. His sister Helen had died the year before, and he made a point of spending part of every evening with his family, joining in their singing. In the fall, he traveled to Quebec with Ellery Channing, and his essay on their journey was serialized in *Putnam's Monthly* as "A Yankee in Canada." When the editor asked Thoreau to remove his criticisms of orthodox religious who "have their scheme of the universe all cut and dried," he refused and the serialization was canceled.

During this period, Thoreau's relationship with Emerson began to deteriorate. Emerson had grown impatient with Thoreau, disappointed at how little he had produced despite his talent. Thoreau in turn increasingly viewed Emerson as patronizing. Moreover, Emerson's literary powers were waning, just as Thoreau was coming into his own as a writer. In fact, Thoreau had outgrown his dependency upon Emerson and required some distance from his longtime mentor for his talent to flourish. Their estrangement lasted for some years, but they eventually reconciled, developing a more appropriate relationship as friends and colleagues rather than as teacher and disciple.

COMMUNICATIONS FROM THE GODS 1851–1862

On July 12, 1851, Thoreau turned thirty-four, well into his middle years at a time when the average lifespan for an American male was less than forty-five years. He had recently been fitted with false teeth, his first book had failed, his lecturing career had stalled, and he was feeling his age. "Here I am thirty-four years old, and yet my life is almost wholly unexpanded," he lamented in his journal at the time. "There is such an interval between my ideal and the actual in many instances that I may say I am unborn."

More troubling even was the decline in the number and intensity of the ecstasies that had visited him so regularly during his earlier years. "I think that no experience which I have today comes up to, or is comparable with, the experiences of my boyhood," he wrote that summer, recalling times when the "earth was the most glorious musical instrument, and I was audience to its strains." But as his ecstasies diminished, he began to give more attention to understanding them, especially the conditions that favored their appearance.[7] Thoreau revisited the Indian scriptures during this period, and his journal entries, copied from the *Harivamsha Purana*, a first-century scriptural text, focus on the ascetic practices that are foundational to Indian spirituality. "Let the spirit, though clogged by the bonds of the body, prepare for itself an abode sure and permanent," he quotes in his journal. The "Mauni" (seeker) should take care "evening and morning to subdue his senses, to fix his mind on the divine essence"—injunctions Thoreau had intuitively translated into his daily regimen. "I find that I conciliate the gods by some sacrament as bathing or abstemiousness in diet, or rising early," he observed while at Walden, "and directly they smile on me. These are my sacraments."

Thoreau was most likely a lifelong celibate who embraced his bachelorhood and celebrated chastity as especially conducive to spiritual pursuits.[8] Predisposed to an austere lifestyle from his early years, he shared the Indian belief that sensuality and sense restraint were not opposed to one another, but were variant expressions of human generative energy. Properly understood, the ascetic practices described in Indian texts like the *Bhagavad Gita* were intended to sublimate sexual energy—not to extinguish or repress it—and transmute it into spiritualized light.[9] Whether Thoreau borrowed his understanding from his reading of these texts, or had intuited it from his own experience, he shares their interpretation. "By poverty, *i.e.,* simplicity of life," he wrote in his journal in 1857, "I am solidified and crystallized, as a vapor or liquid by cold. It is a singular concentration of strength and energy and flavor. Chastity," he declared emphatically, "is perpetual acquaintance with the All." As inexplicable as such notions would have appeared to nineteenth-century Protestants, habituated to the biblical injunction to go forth and multiply, Thoreau was unapologetic: "They are not ordinary practices which can bring light into the soul," he wrote in spring 1856. And in a letter to Harrison Blake, he acknowledged that "rude and careless as I am, I would fain practice the *yoga* faithfully."

Thoreau also began to expand the time he spent in nature, exploring the woods, meadows, and waterways around Concord with increasing deliberation. He began taking walks at night during the full moon, finding it especially congenial to his contemplative moods. "I am sobered by the moonlight," he wrote in August 1851, since it was "more favorable to meditation than sunlight." He also took more extensive notes, describing the plants and flowers he observed with an exacting attention to detail. "It is only when we forget all our learning that we begin to know," he wrote in 1859, describing an almost Zen-like engagement with nature free of preconceptions. "You must approach the [natural] object totally unprejudiced. You must be aware that no thing is what you have taken it to be. . . . Your greatest success will be simply to perceive that such things are."

While Thoreau's ecstasies undoubtedly diminished in their frequency and intensity during his final decade, they by no means abandoned him altogether. He became particularly sensitive to sound, hearing "kindred vibrations" in the music of the Aeolian harp and the birdsong of the wood thrush: "These things alone remind me of my immortality," he wrote in 1853. "They intoxicate, they charm us. . . . I leave my body in a trance and accompany the zephyr and the fragrance." A few years later, he described an episode where he became entranced by the distant strumming of a guitar: "The way in which I am affected by this faint thrumming," he wrote, "advertises me that there is still some health and immortality in the springs of me. What an elixir is this sound! . . . We attain to a wisdom that passeth understanding." Though more muted and less frequent than the raptures of his youth, ecstasies would continue to visit him unbidden throughout his last decade. "The communications from the gods to us are still deep and sweet indeed," he wrote in 1856, "but scanty and transient—enough only to keep alive the memory of the past."

Walden was published in 1854 and received favorable reviews. Compressing his two years at Walden into a single year, Thoreau created a narrative structure that followed the seasons and gave him room to fully address his concerns about the soul-wasting materialism and superficiality of American life. In its call for a simple, principled life, *Walden* is a kind of "secular scripture," a finely calibrated jeremiad against material excess and its ruination of the natural world, and a *cri de coeur* for a life of "simplicity, independence, magnanimity, and trust" that remains as centrally relevant today, in an age of resource scarcity and global warming, as it was in the middle of the Industrial Revolution.[10]

The success of Walden brought Thoreau enough celebrity that he was invited to conduct a lecture tour of New England cities that lasted until the end of the year. But a mysterious illness struck him during the spring of 1855, draining the strength from his legs and making it difficult to continue his daily walks. He remained virtually bedridden for several months, and his daily journal entries fell to just a sentence or two. He gradually recovered his strength and in October traveled to New Jersey on a surveying project, using the opportunity to visit Walt Whitman, whose *Leaves of Grass* had been published the year before. Thoreau was enchanted with Whitman and carried a copy of his controversial book of poems around Concord, according to Emerson, "like a red flag."

The next July, Thoreau revisited the Maine wilderness on a difficult three-hundred-mile canoe trek through swamps and dense forest in the company of an Indian guide named Joe Polis, whose wilderness skills and stoic demeanor left a permanent impression on him. Thoreau had long been intrigued by American Indians and was collecting material for a book about them at the time of his death. He had almost a thousand Indian artifacts in his collection and had come to believe that the continent's indigenous peoples filled a vital niche between nature and "civilized" man. "The Indian possesses so much intelligence which the white man does not," he wrote to Harrison Blake. "I rejoice to find that intelligence flows in other channels than I knew." An account of his first trip to Maine was serialized in one of the earliest editions of the *Atlantic Monthly* and would be published as *The Maine Woods* shortly after his passing.

In January 1859, Thoreau's father died from a long illness, having been nursed by Henry through his last difficult weeks. Thoreau now assumed the management of the family's pencil-manufacturing business, even returning to New York City to settle his father's accounts. That fall he gained some notoriety for his defense of the abolitionist John Brown who tried to initiate a slave revolt when he seized the army arsenal at Harpers Ferry. Thoreau had met Brown in 1857 and was moved by his unwavering commitment to principle. When Brown was tried for sedition, Thoreau, who abhorred violence, defended him in lectures in Concord and Boston and pleaded, to no avail, for his life. Emerson would later remark that Brown had joined Walt Whitman and Joe Polis, the Indian guide from Maine, in "Thoreau's private pantheon."

For several years, Thoreau had studied the natural history of the Concord woodlands, and in September 1861, he delivered what would be his final lecture, "The Succession of Forest Trees." He published the lecture in the *New York Tribune* to wide acclaim, and his observations are considered a significant contribution to the field. But his study would lead to his undoing. In December, he developed bronchitis after being caught in a rainstorm while counting tree rings, and his condition worsened until he became bedridden with what was most likely pneumonia throughout the winter and spring (he had contracted tuberculosis as a young man and his lungs never fully recovered). In May1861, hoping to regain his health in a dryer climate, he traveled to the Midwest and remained in Minnesota until July. When he returned to Concord, his condition had worsened, and by September he understood that his illness was probably fatal. That month he made his last visit to Walden Pond with Sophia, and in November made the final entry in his journal. His health deteriorated further as the winter set in, and by December a permanent flush had appeared on his cheeks, "painful to behold." By the beginning of 1862, Bronson Alcott wrote that his longtime transcendentalist colleague and friend was "fading from our sight."

Despite his condition, Thoreau busied himself with his writing, preparing essays for publication—dictating his thoughts to Sophia when he no longer had the strength to write—while negotiating with his publisher to reprint *Walden*.[11] Friends and neighbors visited, recollecting afterwards how serene and cheerful Thoreau appeared throughout his ordeal. Sam Staples, Thoreau's jailer in 1845, told Emerson afterward that he had never spent an hour "with more satisfaction," had never seen a man dying "with so much pleasure and peace." For his part, Thoreau was moved by the affection that poured in and regretted that he had been so standoffish with his fellow townspeople. When asked by his Aunt Luisa if he had made his peace with God, Thoreau famously remarked, "I did not know we ever quarreled, Aunt."

His serenity was infectious. Most of those that visited did not know how seriously ill he was, as he routinely appeared "so full of life and good cheer." The room did not feel like a sickroom, his mother would remark later. "My son wanted flowers and pictures and books all around here; and he was always so cheerful and wished others to be so while about him." Sophia was more emphatic: "I never before saw such a manifestation of the power of spirit over matter. Very often I have heard him tell his visitors that he enjoyed existence as well as ever." He told Sophia that he found as much comfort in "perfect disease as in perfect health," and the thought of death "could not begin to trouble him." Sophia later recalled that she never heard Thoreau express "the slightest wish to remain." He refused opiates, telling Ellery Channing that he preferred to endure his pain with a clear mind, rather than be plunged into a narcotic dream. His greatest disappointment was that he would be unable to observe the unfolding of spring. By April, Thoreau could speak only in a whisper and remarked to Channing, regarding his impending death, "It is better. Some things should end."

In *Walden* Thoreau had written about his ability to enter a state of detachment that removed his consciousness from his physical self, "a certain doubleness" of awareness, in which, he wrote, "I can stand as remote from myself as from another." And it appears from contemporaneous accounts of his final weeks that he had found his way into just such a state of physical detachment, withdrawing his awareness from the searing agony in his lungs. Even earlier, he had written in his journal, "We need only to retreat further within us to preserve uninterrupted the continuity of serene hours to the end of our lives." By all accounts, his serenity had indeed remained "uninterrupted" through the final difficult weeks of his illness. "He seemed to be in an exalted state of mind for a long time before his death," one friend wrote: "He said it was just as good to be sick as to be well, just as good to have a poor time as a good time." Thoreau had achieved such a palpable detachment from his physical discomfort that the very "wasting away" of his body, according to Channing, seemed to Thoreau a "foreign" event, a development in which he himself "had no hand." Thoreau told Channing that it was in fact possible to view oneself as "a third person," perhaps hinting at his state of consciousness at the end.

Though Thoreau remained unapologetically irreligious until the very end, his final days are lit with an exalted, even sacred dimension we associate with the passing of more overtly religious figures. For Channing, Thoreau's closest friend and confidante, the otherworldly peace and composure of his final days remained beyond expression. "Words," he wrote, "could no longer express the inexplicable conditions of his existence."

Thoreau died on the evening of May 7, 1862, with his mother, his sister Sophia, and his aunt Louisa nearby. "I feel as if something very beautiful had happened," Sophia would say—"not death."[12]

1

The Streams of My Life
Journal and Letters

Thoreau was a passionate spiritual seeker throughout his life, and experienced rapturous, transcendent "ecstasies" from his early youth. But because of a temperamental reluctance to disclose his interior life, and his belief that the interior spiritual life was, for the most part, beyond words, descriptions of his spiritual struggles, practices, concerns, and experience are rarely found in his books and essays. More revealing remarks regarding his spiritual self can be found in the journal he kept from the age of twenty to a few months before his death. The journal, which amounted to more than two million words, was first published in its entirety in 1906, and a revised edition that included newly discovered material was published by Princeton University in eight volumes between 1981 and 2002.

Another source for insight into Thoreau's spiritual concerns, including revelatory remarks about his own inner struggles, is the collection of forty-nine extant letters he wrote to Harrison Otis Blake, a contemporary of Thoreau, who had asked him to serve as a spiritual mentor. (See the introduction for more details.) Thoreau's correspondence with Blake was not published in a separate edition until 2004.

HEAVEN IS THE INMOST PLACE
1837–1842

Thoreau graduated from Harvard in 1837, the same year he began his journal. He and his younger brother, John, ran their own school for three years, beginning in 1839, and during this time Thoreau became friends with Ralph Waldo Emerson, who published his early poems and articles in his transcendentalist journal, The Dial. *In September 1839, John and Henry spent ten days on the Concord and Merrimack rivers, and in 1840, both brothers made unsuccessful proposals of marriage to Ellen Sewall. In 1841, Thoreau was invited to live in Emerson's home, working as a tutor, editorial assistant on* The Dial, *and handyman. In 1842, John Thoreau died of a tetanus infection, plunging Henry into a severe depression.*

October 22, 1837

"What are you doing now?" he asked. "Do you keep a journal?" So I make my first entry today.

To be alone I find it necessary to escape the present—I avoid myself. How could I be alone in the Roman emperor's chamber of mirrors? I seek a garret. The spiders must not be disturbed, nor the floor swept, nor the lumber arranged. —JOU i, 3

October 27, 1837

The prospect is limited to [Mounts] Nobscot and Annursnack. The trees stand with boughs downcast like pilgrims beaten by a storm, and the whole landscape wears a somber aspect.

So when thick vapors cloud the soul, it strives in vain to escape from its humble working-day valley, and pierce the dense fog which shuts out from view the blue peaks in its horizon, but must be content to scan its near and homely hills. —JOU i, 6

November 5, 1837

Truth strikes us from behind, and in the dark, as well as from before and in broad daylight. —JOU i, 8

November 12, 1837

I yet lack discernment to distinguish the whole lesson of today; but it is not lost—it will come to me at last. My desire is to know *what* I have lived, that I may know *how* to live henceforth.

—JOU i, 9

January 21, 1838

Every leaf and twig was this morning covered with a sparkling ice armor. . . . It was as though some superincumbent stratum of the earth had been removed in the night, exposing to light a bed of untarnished crystals. . . . There were the opal and sapphire and emerald and jasper and beryl and topaz and ruby.

Such is beauty ever—neither here nor there, now nor then—neither in Rome nor in Athens, but wherever there is a soul to admire. If I seek her elsewhere because I do not find her at home, my search will prove a fruitless one. —JOU i, 26

August 10, 1838

The human soul is a silent harp in God's choir, whose strings need only to be swept by the divine breath to chime in with the harmonies of creation. Every pulse-beat is in exact time with the cricket's chant, and the tickings of the deathwatch in the wall. Alternate with these if you can. —JOU i, 53

May 21, 1839

Who knows how incessant a surveillance a strong man may maintain over himself—how far subject [his] passion and appetite to reason, and lead the life his imagination paints?. . . By a strong effort may he not command even his brute body in unconscious moments? —JOU i, 79

June 22, 1839

I have within the last few days come into contact with a pure, uncompromising spirit, that is somewhere wandering in the atmosphere, but settles not positively anywhere. Some persons carry about them the air and conviction of virtue, though they themselves are unconscious of it. . . . Such it is impossible not to love; still is their loveliness, as it were, independent of them, so that you seem not to lose it when they are absent, for when they are near it is like an invisible presence which attends you.

—JOU i, 80

July 25, 1839

There is no remedy for love but to love more. —JOU i, 88

September 13, 1839

I never feel that I am inspired unless my body is also. It too spurns a tame and commonplace life. They are fatally mistaken who think while they strive with their minds, that they may suffer their bodies to stagnate in luxury or sloth. The body is the first proselyte the Soul makes. Our life is but the Soul made known by its fruits—the body. The whole duty of man may be expressed in one line—Make to yourself a perfect body. — PJ i, 137–38

March 21, 1840

Our limbs, indeed, have room enough, but it is our souls that rust in a corner. Let us migrate interiorly without intermission, and pitch our tent each day nearer the western horizon. —JOU i, 131

April 19, 1840

The infinite bustle of Nature of a summer's noon, or her infinite silence of a summer's night, gives utterance to no dogma. They do not say to us even with a seer's assurance, that this or that law is immutable and so ever and only can the universe exist. But they are the indifferent occasion for all things and the annulment of all laws. —JOU i, 133

April 22, 1840

Thales was the first of the Greeks who taught that souls are immortal, and it takes equal wisdom to discern this old fact today. What the first philosopher taught, the last will have to repeat. The *world* makes no progress. —JOU i, 134

June 23, 1840

I cannot see the bottom of the sky, because I cannot see to the bottom of myself. It is the symbol of my own infinity. My eye penetrates as far into the ether as that depth is inward from which my contemporary thought springs.

Not by constraint or severity shall you have access to true wisdom, but by abandonment, and childlike mirthfulness. If you would know aught, be gay before it. —JOU i, 150

July 2, 1840

I am not taken up, like Moses, upon a mountain to learn the law, but lifted up in my seat here, in the warm sunshine and genial light. —JOU i, 158

July 6, 1840

Have no mean hours, but be grateful for every hour, and accept what it brings. The reality will make any sincere record respectable. No day will have been wholly misspent, if one sincere, thoughtful page has been written.

Let the daily tides leave some deposit on these pages, as it leaves sand and shells on the shore. So much increase of terra firma. This may be a calendar of the ebbs and flows of the soul; and on these sheets as a beach, the waves may cast up pearls and seaweed. —JOU i, 162–63

January 23, 1841

When I detect a beauty in any of the recesses of nature, I am reminded by the serene and retired spirit in which it requires to be contemplated, of the inexpressible privacy of a life—how silent and unambitious it is. The beauty there is in mosses will have to be considered from the holiest, quietest nook. The gods delight in stillness; they say, "St—st." My truest, serenest moments are too still for emotion. They have woolen feet. In all our lives we live under the hill, and if we are not gone we live there still.

—JOU i, 174

January 30, 1841

These particles of snow which the early wind shakes down are what is stirring, or the morning news of the wood. Sometimes it is blown up above the trees, like the sand of the desert.

You glance up these paths, closely imbowered by bent trees, as through the side aisles of a cathedral, and expect to hear a choir chanting from their depths. You are never so far in them as they are far before you. Their secret is where you are not and where your feet can never carry you. —JOU i, 184–85

February 7, 1841

The eaves are running on the south side of the house; the titmouse lisps in the poplar; the bells are ringing for church; while the sun presides over all and makes his simple warmth more obvious than all else. What shall I do with this hour, so like time and yet so fit for eternity? Where in me are these russet patches of ground, and scattered logs and chips in the yard? I do not feel cluttered. I have some notion what the John's-wort and Life-everlasting may be thinking about when the sun shines on me as on them and turns my prompt thought into just such a seething shimmer. I lie out indistinct as a heath at noonday. I am evaporating and ascending into the sun. —JOU i, 203–4

February 8, 1841

My journal is that of me which would else spill over and run to waste, gleanings from the field which in action I reap. I must not live for it, but in it for the gods. They are my correspondent, to whom daily I send off this sheet postpaid. I am clerk in their counting-room, and at evening transfer the account from day-book to ledger. It is as a leaf which hangs over my head in the path. I bend the twig and write my prayers on it; then letting it go, the bough springs up and shows the scrawl to heaven.

—JOU i, 206–7

February 14, 1841

I am confined to the house by bronchitis, and so seek to content myself with that quiet and serene life there is in a warm corner by the fireside, and see the sky through the chimney-top. Sickness should not be allowed to extend further than the body. We need only to retreat further within us to preserve uninterrupted the continuity of serene hours to the end of our lives. . . .

I shall never be poor while I can command a still hour in which to take leave of my sin. —JOU i, 214

February 15, 1841

There is elevation in every hour. No part of the earth is so low and withdrawn that the heavens cannot be seen from it, but every part supports the sky. We have only to stand on the eminence of the hour, and look out thence into the empyrean, allowing no pinnacle above us, to command an uninterrupted horizon. The moments will be outspread around us like a blue expanse of mountain and valley, while we stand on the summit of our hour as if we had descended on eagle's wings. —JOU i, 214–15

May 27, 1841

I sit in my boat on Walden, playing the flute this evening, and see the perch, which I seem to have charmed, hovering around me, and the moon traveling over the bottom, which is strewn with the wrecks of the forest, and feel that nothing but the wildest imagination can conceive of the manner of life we are living. Nature is a wizard. The Concord nights are stranger than the Arabian nights.

We not only want elbow-room, but eye-room in this gray air which shrouds all the fields. Sometimes my eyes see over the county road by daylight to the tops of yonder birches on the hill, as at others by moonlight.

Heaven lies above, because the air is deep.

In all my life hitherto I have left nothing behind. —JOU i, 260–61

May 31, 1841

That title, "The Laws of Manu," [first-century Indian text] comes to me with such a volume of sound as if it had swept unobstructed over the plains of Hindostan; and when my eye rests on yonder birches, or the sun in the water, or the shadows of the trees, it seems to signify the laws of them all. They are the laws of you and me, a fragrance wafted down from those old times, and no more to be refuted than the wind.

When my imagination travels eastward and backward to those remote years of the gods, I seem to draw near to the habitation of the morning, and the dawn at length has a place. I remember the book as an hour before sunrise.

We are height and depth both, a calm sea at the foot of a promontory. Do we not overlook our own depths? —JOU i, 261

August 1, 1841

The best thought is not only without somberness, but even without morality. . . . Occasionally we rise above the necessity of virtue into an unchangeable morning light, in which we have not to choose in a dilemma between right and wrong, but simply to live right on and breathe the circumambient air. There is no name for this life unless it be the very vitality of *vita*. Silent is the preacher about this, and silent must ever be, for he who knows it will not preach. —JOU i, 265

August 18, 1841

I sailed on the North River last night with my flute, and my music was a tinkling stream which meandered with the river, and fell from note to note as a brook from rock to rock. I did not hear the strains after they had issued from the flute, but before they were breathed into it, for the original strain precedes the sound by as much as the echo follows after, and the rest is the perquisite of the rocks and trees and beasts. Unpremeditated music is the true gauge which measures the current of our thoughts, the very undertow of our life's stream. —JOU i, 271–72

September 1, 1841

Let us know and conform only to the fashions of eternity.
—JOU i, 278

September 2, 1841

There is but one obligation and that is the obligation to obey the highest dictate. None can lay me under another which will supersede this. The gods have given me these years without any encumbrance; society has no mortgage on them. If any man assist me in the way of the world, let him derive satisfaction from the deed itself, for I think I never shall have dissolved my prior obligations to God. —JOU i, 279

December 24, 1841

I want to go soon and live away by the pond, where I shall hear only the wind whispering among the reeds. It will be success if I shall have left myself behind. But my friends ask what I will do when I get there. Will it not be employment enough to watch the progress of the seasons? —JOU i, 299

December 25, 1841

I don't want to feel as if my life were a sojourn any longer. That philosophy cannot be true which so paints it. It is time now that I begin to live. —JOU i, 299

December 29, 1841

Heaven is the inmost place. The good have not to travel far. What cheer may we not derive from the thought that our courses do not diverge, and we wend not asunder, but as the web of destiny is woven it [is] fulled, and we are cast more and more into the center! . . .

I wish I could be as still as God is. I can recall to my mind the stillest summer hour, in which the grasshopper sings over the mulleins, and there is a valor in that time the memory of which is armor that can laugh at any blow of fortune. . . .

I would be as clean as ye, O woods. I shall not rest till I be as innocent as you. I know that I shall sooner or later attain to an unspotted innocence, for when I consider that state even now I am thrilled. . . . These motions everywhere in nature must surely [be] the circulations of God. The flowing sail, the running stream, the waving tree, the roving wind—whence else their infinite health and freedom? I can see nothing so proper and holy as unrelaxed play and frolic in this bower God has built for us. The suspicion of sin never comes to this thought. —JOU i, 301–2

January 1, 1842

Virtue is the deed of the bravest. It is that art which demands the greatest confidence and fearlessness. Only some hardy soul ventures upon it. Virtue is a bravery so hardy that it deals in what it has no experience in. The virtuous soul possesses a fortitude and hardihood which not the grenadier nor pioneer can match. It never shrunk. It goes singing to its work. Effort is its relaxation. The rude pioneer work of this world has been done by the most devoted worshippers of beauty. Their resolution has possessed a keener edge than the soldier's. In winter is their campaign; they never go into quarters. They are elastic under the heaviest burden, under the extremest physical suffering. —JOU i, 308

Thoreau's brother, John, died of lockjaw on January 11, 1842, followed two weeks later by six-year-old Waldo Emerson, Thoreau's favorite, who died of scarlet fever. The shock to Thoreau was profound. He experienced a sympathetic version of lockjaw, was bedridden for weeks, and was haunted by John's death for years.

February 20, 1842

My path hitherto has been like a road through a diversified country, now climbing high mountains, then descending into the lowest vales. From the summits I saw the heavens; from the vales I looked up to the heights again. In prosperity I remember God, or memory, is one with consciousness; in adversity I remember my own elevations, and only hope to see God again. —JOU i, 320

February 21, 1842

I was always conscious of sounds in nature which my ears could never hear—that I caught but the prelude to a strain. She always retreats as I advance. Away behind and behind is she and her meaning. Will not this faith and expectation make to itself ears at length? I never saw to the end, nor heard to the end; but the best part was unseen and unheard.

I am like a feather floating in the atmosphere; on every side is depth unfathomable.

I feel as if years had been crowded into the last month. . . .

I have lived ill for the most part because too near myself. I have tripped myself up, so that there was no progress for my own narrowness. I cannot walk conveniently and pleasantly but when I hold myself far off in the horizon. And the soul dilutes the body and makes it passable. My soul and body have tottered along together of late, tripping and hindering one another like unpracticed Siamese twins. They two should walk as one, that no obstacle may be nearer than the firmament.

There must be some narrowness in the soul that compels one to have secrets. —JOU i, 321–22

March 1, 1842

Whatever I learn from any circumstances, that especially I needed to know. Events come out of God, and our characters determine them and constrain fate, as much as they determine the words and tone of a friend to us. Hence are they always acceptable as experience, and we do not see how we could have done without them. —JOU i, 323–24

March 2, 1842

Only nature has a right to grieve perpetually, for she only is innocent. Soon the ice will melt, and the blackbirds sing along the river which he [John] frequented, as pleasantly as ever. The same everlasting serenity will appear in this face of God, and we will not be sorrowful, if he is not. —Letter to Lucy Brown, COR, 62–63

March 11, 1842

How plain that death is only the phenomenon of the individual or class. Nature does not recognize it, she finds her own again under new forms without loss. Yet death is beautiful when seen to be a law, and not an accident—It is as common as life. . . .

Every blade in the field, every leaf in the forest, lays down its life in its season as beautifully as it was taken up. . . . Dead trees—sere leaves—dried grass and herbs—are not these a good part of our life?

—Letter to Emerson, COR, 64–65

March 11, 1842

If Nature is our mother, is not God much more? God should come into our thoughts with no more parade than the zephyr into our ears. Only strangers approach him with ceremony. How rarely in our English tongue do we find expressed any affection for God! The Protestant Church seems to have nothing to supply the place of the saints of the Catholic calendar, who were at least channels for the affections. Its God has perhaps too many of the attributes of a Scandinavian deity.

We can only live healthily the life the gods assign us. I must receive my life as passively as the willow leaf that flutters over the brook. I must not be for myself, but God's work, and that is always good. I will wait the breezes patiently, and grow as Nature shall determine. . . .

My life, my life! Why will you linger? Are the years short and the months of no account? How often has long delay quenched my aspirations! Can God afford that I should forget him? Is he so indifferent to my career? Can heaven be postponed with no more ado? Why were my ears given to hear those everlasting strains which haunt my life, and yet to be profaned much more by these perpetual dull sounds?

—JOU i, 326–27

March 14, 1842

Love never stands still, nor does its object. It is the revolving sun and the swelling bud. If I know what I love, it is because I remember it.

Life is grand, and so are its environments of Past and Future. Would the face of nature be so serene and beautiful if man's destiny were not equally so? What am I good for now, who am still marching after high things, but to hear and tell the news, to bring wood and water, and count how many eggs the hens lay? In the meanwhile, I expect my life will begin. I will not aspire longer. I will see what it is I would be after. —JOU i, 330

March 17, 1842

I have been making pencils all day, and then at evening walked to see an old schoolmate who is going to help make the Welland Canal navigable for ships round Niagara. He cannot see any such motives and modes of living as I; professes not to look beyond the securing of certain "creature comforts." And so we go silently different ways, with all serenity, I in the still moonlight through the village this fair evening to write these thoughts in my journal, and he, forsooth, to mature his schemes to ends as good, maybe, but different. So are we two made, while the same stars shine quietly over us. If I or he be wrong, Nature yet consents placidly. She bites her lip and smiles to see how her children will agree. So does the Welland Canal get built, and other conveniences, while I live. Well and good, I must confess. —JOU i, 335

April 3, 1842

I have just heard the flicker among the oaks on the hillside ushering in a new dynasty. It is the age and youth of time. Why did Nature set this lure for sickly mortals? Eternity could not begin with more security and momentousness than the spring. The summer's eternity is reestablished by this note. All sights and sounds are seen and heard both in time and eternity. . . .

The destiny of the soul can never be studied by the reason, for its modes are not ecstatic. In the wisest calculation or demonstration I but play a game with myself. I am not to be taken captive by myself.

I cannot convince myself. God must convince. I can calculate a problem in arithmetic, but not any morality.

Virtue is incalculable, as it is inestimable. Well, man's destiny is but virtue, or manhood. It is wholly moral, to be learned only by the life of the soul. . . .

On one side of man is the actual, and on the other the ideal. The former is the province of the reason; it is even a divine light when directed upon it, but it cannot reach forward into the ideal without blindness. The moon was made to rule by night, but the sun to rule by day. Reason will be but a pale cloud, like the moon, when one ray of divine light comes to illumine the soul.

—JOU i, 359–60

THE PRESENCE OF MY KINDRED
1843–1850

Following the death of his brother and concerned that his poetry was drying up, Thoreau appears to have experienced an emotional low point in 1843. He moved to Staten Island in New York to serve as a tutor for the son of Emerson's brother and to make his way in the New York literary world. He failed to interest a publisher in his writing, but Horace Greeley, the editor of the New York Tribune, *became a mentor and informal literary agent who would help Thoreau publish his articles. While in Staten Island, Thoreau suffered from homesickness and found New York City deeply distasteful. He moved back to Concord at the end of the year and joined his father in his pencil business. He managed to publish several articles during the next two years and gave an occasional lecture at the Concord Lyceum. In July 1845, he moved to Walden Pond, where he lived for two years as an experiment in simple living and wrote drafts for what would become his first book,* A Week on the Concord and Merrimack Rivers, *and his masterpiece,* Walden.

Thoreau left Walden in September 1847 and moved back into Emerson's house to look after his family while the latter toured

Europe on a lecture tour. In 1848 Thoreau published his description of a journey he took to the Maine woods, and in July moved into his parents' home. He began surveying as a means of earning a living and started lecturing professionally. In 1849 he published A Week on the Concord and Merrimack Rivers *as well as the essay that would become "Civil Disobedience." In 1850 he traveled to Cape Cod, New York City, and Quebec.*

November 2, 1843

I believe that there is an ideal or real nature, infinitely more perfect than the actual, as there is an ideal life of man. Else, where are the glorious summers which in vision sometimes visit my brain?

When nature ceases to be supernatural to a man, what will he do? Of what worth is human life, if its actions are no longer to have this sublime and unexplored scenery? Who will build a cottage and dwell in it with enthusiasm, if not in the Elysian fields?
—PJ i, 481

July 7, 1845

The Great Spirit makes indifferent all times and places. The place where he is seen is always the same, and indescribably pleasant to all our senses. We had allowed only neighboring and transient circumstances to make our occasions. . . . But nearest to all things is that power which fashions its being. Next to us the grandest laws are being enacted and administered. —JOU i, 363–64

July 14, 1845

Sometimes, when I compare myself with other men, methinks I am favored by the gods. They seem to whisper joy to me beyond my deserts, and that I do have a solid warrant and surety at their hands, which my fellows do not. I do not flatter myself, but if it were possible they flatter me. I am especially guided and guarded.
—JOU i, 365

August 23, 1845

I would not forget that I deal with infinite and divine qualities in my fellow. All men indeed are divine in their core of light, but that is indistinct and distant to me, like the stars of the least magnitude—or the galaxy itself. . . . —PJ ii, 175–77

After April 18, 1846

The struggle in me is between a lover of contemplation and a love of action—the life of a philosopher and of a hero. The poetic and philosophic have my constant vote. The practic [sic] hinders and unfits me for the former. . . .

To make a perfect man, the soul must be much like the body, not too unearthly, and the body like the soul. The one must not deny and oppress the other.

For the most part I know not how the hours go. Certainly I am not living that heroic life I had dreamed of. And yet all my things are full of life, and nature whispers no reproach. The day advances as if to light some work of mine, and I defer in my thought as if there were somewhere busier men. It was morning, and lo! It is now evening. And nothing memorable is accomplished. Yet my nature is almost content with this. Here's no reproach in nature.

What are these pines and these birds about? What is this pond a-doing? I must know a little more, and be forever ready. Instead of singing as the birds, I silently smile at my incessant good fortune, but I don't know that I bear any flowers or fruits. Methinks if they try me by their standards, I shall not be found wanting. . . .

I think I have this advantage in my present mode of life over those who are obliged to look abroad for amusement—to theaters and society—that my life itself is my amusement and never ceases to be novel—the commencement of an experiment, or drama which will never end. —PJ ii, 240–42

June 20, 1846

When my friends reprove me for not devoting myself to some trade or profession, and acquiring property, I feel not the reproach. I am guiltless and safe comparatively on that score. . . . But I am advised by the friend of friends, to strive singly for the highest—without concern for the lower. The integrity of life is otherwise sacrificed to factitious virtues. . . .When I am reproved for being what I am, I find the only resource is being still more entirely what I am.

—PJ ii, 248–49

Thoreau received a letter from Harrison Blake in March 1848 requesting that they correspond with each other. (See the introduction for a fuller treatment of Blake's request.) Below is Thoreau's response to Blake's request, which began a correspondence that would continue until shortly before Thoreau's death in 1862.

March 27, 1848

Mr. Blake—

I am glad to hear that any words of mine, though spoken so long ago that I can hardly claim identity with their author, have reached you. It gives me pleasure, because I have therefore reason to suppose that I have uttered what concerns men, and that is not in vain that man speaks to man. This is the value of literature. . . .

I do believe that the outward and the inward life correspond; that if any should succeed to live a higher life, others would not know of it; that difference and distance are one. To set about living a true life is to go [on] a journey to a distant country, gradually to find ourselves surrounded by new scenes and men; and as long as the old are around me, I know that I am not in any true sense living a new or a better life. The outward is only the outside of that which is within. . . .

I do believe in simplicity. It is astonishing as well as sad, how many trivial affairs even the wisest man thinks he must attend to in a day; how singular an affair he thinks he must omit. . . . So simplify the problem of life, distinguish the necessary and the real. Probe the earth to see where your main roots run. . . .

This, our respectable daily life, in which the man of common sense, the Englishman of the world, stands so squarely, and on which our institutions are founded, is in fact the veriest illusion, and will vanish like the baseless fabric of a vision; but that faint glimmer of reality which sometimes illuminates the darkness of daylight for all men, reveals something more solid and enduring than adamant, which is in fact the cornerstone of the world. . . .

I have no designs on society—or nature—or God. I am simply what I am, or I begin to be that. I *live* in the *present*. I only remember the past—and anticipate the future. I love to live, I love reform better than its modes. There is no history of how bad became better. I believe something, and there is nothing else but that. I know that I am . . . I know that the enterprise is worthy—I know that things work well. I have heard no bad news. . . .

Pursue, keep up with, circle round and round your life as a dog does his master's chaise. Do what you love. Know your own bone; gnaw at it, bury it, unearth it, and gnaw it still. Do not be too moral. You may cheat yourself out of much life so. Aim above morality. Be not *simply* good—be good for something. . . .

Let nothing come between you and the light. Respect men as brothers only. When you travel to the celestial city, carry no letter of introduction. When you knock ask to see God—none of the servants. In what concerns you much do not think that you have companions—know that you are alone in the world.

—Letter to Harrison Blake, LSS, 36–39

May 2, 1848

Mr. Blake—

You ask if there is no doctrine of sorrow in my philosophy. Of acute sorrow, I suppose that I know comparatively little. My saddest and most genuine sorrows are apt to be but transient regrets. . . . In my cheapest moments I am apt to think that it is not my business to be "seeking the spirit," but as much its business to be seeking me. . . . I am too easily contented with a slight and almost animal happiness. My happiness is a good deal like that of the woodchucks.

—Letter to Harrison Blake, LSS, 43

After July 30, 1848

I find that I conciliate the gods by some sacrament as bathing or abstemiousness in diet, or rising early—and directly they smile on me. These are my sacraments. — PJ iii, 4

August 10, 1849

Mr. Blake—

Happy the man who observes the heavenly and the terrestrial law in just proportion; whose every faculty, from the soles of his feet to the crown of his head, obeys the law of its level; who neither stoops nor goes on tiptoe, but lives a balanced life, acceptable to nature and to God.

These things I say; other things I do.

—Letter to Harrison Blake, LSS, 47

By November 1849, it was clear that A Week on the Concord and Merrimack Rivers *had failed, incurring a debt for Thoreau of $300. As a result, he spent long hours in his family's pencil factory and increased his surveying work. Largely because of the improvements Thoreau made in the manufacturing process, his father's business flourished, allowing the family to build a new home on Main Street in Concord. In 1850, Thoreau moved into the attic where he would live for the rest of his life.*

November 20, 1849

Mr. Blake—

I have not forgotten that I am your debtor. When I read over your letters, as I have just done, I feel that I am unworthy to have received or to answer them, though they are addressed, as I would have them to the ideal of me. It behooves me, if I would reply, to speak out of the rarest part of myself. . . .

Within a year my walks have extended themselves, and in almost every afternoon (I read, or write, or make pencils in the forenoon, and by the last means get a living for my body) I visit some new hill or pond or wood many miles distant. . . .

"Free in this world, as the birds in the air, disengaged from every kind of chains, those who have practiced the *yoga* gather in Brahma the certain fruit of their works."

Depend upon it that rude and careless as I am, I would fain practice the *yoga* faithfully.

"The yogin, absorbed in contemplation, contributes in his degree to creation: he breathes a divine perfume, he hears wonderful things. Divine forms traverse him without tearing him, and united to the nature which is proper to him, he goes, he acts, as animating original matter." To some extent, and at rare intervals, even I am a yogin. —Letter to Harrison Blake, LSS, 49–50

April 3, 1850

Mr. Blake—

I thank you for your letter and I will endeavor to record some of the thoughts which it suggests, whether pertinent or not. You speak of poverty and dependence. Who are poor and dependent? Who are the rich and independent? When was it that men agreed to respect the appearance and not the reality? . . . How sweet it would be to treat men and things, for an hour, just for what they are! . . . When we are weary with travel, we lay down our load and rest by the wayside. So, when we are weary with the burden of life, why do we not lay down this load of falsehoods which we have volunteered to sustain, and be refreshed as never mortal was? Let the beautiful laws prevail. Let us not weary ourselves by resisting them. When we would rest our bodies we cease to support them; we recline on the lap of Earth. So, when we would rest our spirits, we must recline on the Great Spirit. . . .

Let God alone if need be. Methinks, if I loved him more, I should keep him—I should keep myself rather—at a more respectful distance. It is not when I am going to meet him, but when I am just turning away and leaving him alone, that I discover that God is. I say, God. I am not sure that that is the name. You will know what I mean. . . .

—Letter to Harrison Blake, LSS, 52–54

May 12(?), 1850

The Hindus are more serenely and thoughtfully religious than the Hebrews. They have perhaps a purer, more independent and impersonal knowledge of God. Their religious books describe the first inquisitive and contemplative access to God; the Hebrew Bible a conscientious return, a grosser and more personal repentance. Repentance is not a free and fair highway to God. A wise man will dispense with repentance. It is shocking and passionate. God prefers that you approach him thoughtful, not penitent, though you are the chief of sinners. It is only by forgetting yourself that you draw near to him. —JOU ii, 3

After July 29, 1850

This stream of events which we consent to call actual, and that other mightier stream which alone carries us with it—what makes the difference? On the one our bodies float, and we have sympathy with it through them; on the other, our spirits.

We are ever dying to one world and being born into another, and possibly no man knows whether he is at any time dead in the sense in which he affirms that phenomenon of another, or not. Our thoughts are the epochs of our life: all else is but as a journal of the winds that blew while we were here.

I do not think much of the actual. —JOU ii, 3–4

In early August Margaret Fuller, a brilliant early feminist and transcendentalist, drowned with her family near Fire Island in New York when their steamer went aground. Their bodies were not recovered, and Emerson asked Thoreau to travel to New York to search the site of the wreck for her effects.

August 9, 1850

Mr. Blake—

I received your letter just as I was rushing to Fire Island beach to recover what remained of Margaret Fuller and read it on the way. That event and its train, as much as anything, have prevented my answering it before. It is wisest to speak when you are spoken to. I will now endeavor to reply at the risk of having nothing to say.

I find that actual events, notwithstanding the singular prominence which we allow them, are far less real than the creations of my imagination. They are truly visionary and insignificant—all that we commonly call life and death—and affect me less than my dreams. . . .

As for conforming outwardly, and living your own life inwardly, I do not think much of that. Let not your right hand know what your left hand does in that line of business. . . . It is a greater strain than any soul can long endure. When you get God to pulling one way and the Devil the other, each having his feet well braced—to say nothing of the conscience sawing transversely—almost any timber will give way.

—Letter to Harrison Blake, LSS, 59–62

October 17, 1850

Cultivate poverty like sage, like a garden herb. Do not trouble yourself to get new things, whether clothes or friends. That is dissipation. . . . If I were confined to a corner in a garret all my days like a spider, the world would be just as large to me, while I had my thoughts.

—PJ iii, 122

November 16, 1850

What shall we do with a man who is afraid of the woods, their solitude and darkness? What salvation is there for him? God is silent and mysterious.

—JOU ii, 100

November 21, 1850

I saw the sun falling on a distant white pine wood whose gray and moss-covered stems were visible amid the green, in an angle where this forest abutted on a hill covered with shrub oaks. It was like looking into dreamland. It is one of the avenues to my future. Certain coincidences like this are accompanied by a certain flash as of hazy lightning, flooding all the world suddenly with the tremulous serene light which it is difficult to see long at a time.

I saw Fair Haven Pond with its island, and meadow between the island and the shore, and a strip of perfectly still and smooth water in the lee of the island, and two hawks, fish hawks perhaps, sailing over it. I did not see how it could be improved. Yet I do not see what these things can be. I begin to see such an object when I cease to *understand* it and see that I did not realize or appreciate it before, but I get no further than this.

—JOU ii, 106–7

November 25, 1850

Just as the sun shines into us warmly and serenely, our Creator breathes on us and re-creates us.

—JOU ii, 112

TRACES OF THE INEFFABLE 1851

During the summer Thoreau lamented the decline he had experienced in his ecstatic episodes, both in their regularity and intensity. The Fugitive Slave Act had become law the year before, and as a result, Thoreau intensified his participation in the Underground Railroad, helping escaped slaves on their way to Canada. His surveying work required more time from him than he wanted, but it was essential to pay off the debt he had incurred with the failure of A Week. *By the autumn of 1851, Thoreau was able to continue his work on* Walden *and gave lectures on "The Wild" and "Walking," both of which would eventually be published as essays.*

January 5, 1851

Almost all that my neighbors call good I believe in my soul to be bad. If I repent of anything it is of my good behavior. What demon possessed me that I behaved so well? —JOU ii, 137

January 7, 1851

The snow is sixteen inches deep at least, but [it] is a mild and genial afternoon, as if it were the beginning of a January thaw. Take away the snow and it would not be winter but like many days in the fall. The birds acknowledge the difference in the air; the jays are more noisy, and the chickadees are oftener heard. . . .

I must live above all in the present. —JOU ii, 137–38

January 10, 1851

[Perhaps I am more] than usually jealous of my freedom. I feel that my connections with and obligations to society are at present very slight and transient. Those slight labors which afford me a livelihood, and by which I am serviceable to my contemporaries, are as yet a pleasure to me, and I am not often reminded that they are a necessity. So far I am successful, and only he is successful in his business who makes that pursuit which affords him the highest pleasure sustain him. But I foresee that if my wants should be much increased, the labor required to supply them would become a drudgery. If I should sell both my forenoons and afternoons to society, neglecting my peculiar calling, there would be nothing left worth living for. I trust that I shall never thus sell my birthright for a mess of pottage. . . .

It is something to know when you are addressed by Divinity and not by a common traveler. I went down cellar just now to get an armful of wood and, passing the brick piers with my wood and candle, I heard, methought, a commonplace suggestion, but when, as it were by accident, I reverently attended to the hint, I found that it was the voice of a god who had followed me down cellar to speak to me. How many communications may we not lose through inattention!

I would fain keep a journal which should contain those thoughts and impressions which I am most liable to forget that I have had; which would have in one sense the greatest remoteness, in another, the greatest nearness to me. —JOU ii, 141–43

February 16, 1851

Do we call this the land of the free? What is it to be free from King George IV and continue the slaves of prejudice? What is it [to] be born free and equal and not to live? What is the value of any political freedom, but as a means to moral freedom? Is it a freedom to be slaves or freedom to be free, of which we boast? . . . We are provincial, because we do not find at home our standards, because we do not worship truth but the reflection of truth, because we are absorbed in and narrowed by trade and commerce and agriculture, which are but means and not the end.
—JOU ii, 162–63

February 27, 1851

I feel that the man who, in conversation with me about the life of man in New England, lays much stress on railroads, telegraphs, and such enterprises does not go below the surface of things. He treats the shallow and transitory as if it were profound and enduring. . . .

I wish my neighbors were wilder.

A wildness whose glance no civilization could endure.
—JOU ii, 170–71

April 1851

About a week ago the authorities of Boston, having the sympathy of many of the inhabitants of Concord, assembled in the gray of the dawn, assisted by a still larger armed force, to send back a perfectly innocent man, and one whom they knew to be innocent, into a slavery as complete as the world ever knew. . . . They sent him back, I say, to live in slavery with other three millions . . . who do not, like the first mentioned, assert the right to govern themselves, but simply to run away and stay away from their prison house. —JOU ii, 175

May 21, 1851

I think that we are not commonly aware that man is our contemporary—that in this strange, outlandish world, so barren, so prosaic, fit not to live in but merely to pass through, that even here so divine a creature as man does actually live. Man, the crowning fact, the god we know. While the earth supports so rare an inhabitant, there is somewhat to cheer us. Who shall say that there is no God, if there is a *just* man. —JOU ii, 207

June 11, 1851

Last night a beautiful summer night, not too warm, moon not quite full, after two or three rainy days. Walked to Fair Haven (Pond) by railroad, returning by Potter's pasture and Sudbury Road. I feared at first that there would be too much white light, like the pale remains of daylight, and not a yellow, gloomy, dreamier light; that it would be like a candlelight by day; but when I got away from the town and deeper into the night, it was better. I hear whip-poor-wills, and see a few fireflies in the meadow. . . .

Ah, that life that I have known! How hard it is to remember what is most memorable! We remember how we itched, not how our hearts beat. I can sometimes recall to mind the quality, the immortality, of my youthful life, but in memory is the only relation to it. —JOU ii, 234–38

June 13, 1851

Walked to Walden last night (moon not quite full) by railroad and upland wood-path, returning by Wayland Road. . . .

As I approached the pond down Hubbard's Path, after coming out of the woods into a warmer air, I saw the shimmering of the moon on its surface, and, in the near, now flooded cove, the water-bugs, darting, circling about, made streaks or curves of light. . . .

The water shines with an inward light like a heaven on earth. The silent depth and serenity and majesty of water! Strange that men should distinguish gold and diamonds, when these precious elements are so common. . . .

We do not commonly live our life out and full; we do not fill all our pores with our blood; we do not inspire and expire fully and entirely enough, so that the wave, the comber, of each inspiration shall break upon our extremest shores, rolling till it meets the sand which bounds us, and the sound of the surf come back to us. Might not a bellows assist us to breathe? That our breathing should create a wind in a calm day! We live but a fraction of our life. Why do we not let on the flood, raise the gates, and set all our wheels in motion? He that hath ears to hear, let him hear.

—JOU ii, 248–51

June 22, 1851

My pulse must beat with Nature. After a hard day's work without a thought, turning my very brain into a mere tool, only in the quiet of evening do I so far recover my senses as to hear the cricket, which in fact has been chirping all day. In my better hours I am conscious of the influx of a serene and unquestionable wisdom which partly unfits, and if I yielded to it more rememberingly would wholly unfit me for what is called the active business of life, for that furnishes nothing on which the eye of reason can rest. What is that other kind of life to which I am thus continually allured? Which alone I love? Is it a life for this world? Can a man feed and clothe himself gloriously who keeps only the truth steadily before him? Who calls in no evil to his aid? Are there duties which necessarily interfere with the serene perception of truth? Are our serene moments mere foretastes of heaven—joys gratuitously vouchsafed to us as a consolation—or simply a transient realization of what might be the whole tenor of our lives?

—JOU ii, 268–69

July 16, 1851

Methinks my present experience is nothing; my past experience is all in all. I think that no experience which I have today comes up to, or is comparable with, the experiences of my boyhood. And not only this is true, but as far back as I can remember I have unconsciously referred to the experiences of a previous state of existence. "For life is a forgetting," etc. . . . Formerly, methought, nature developed as I developed, and grew up with me. My life was ecstasy. In youth, before I lost any of my senses, I can remember that I was all alive, and inhabited my body with inexpressible satisfaction; both its weariness and its refreshment were sweet to me. This earth was the most glorious musical instrument, and I was audience to its strains. To have such sweet impressions made on us, such ecstasies begotten of the breezes! I can remember how I was astonished. I said to myself—I said to others— "There comes into my mind such an indescribable, infinite, all-absorbing, divine, heavenly pleasure, a sense of elevation and expansion, and [I] have had nought to do with it. I perceive that I am dealt with by superior powers. This is a pleasure, a joy, an existence which I have not procured myself. I speak as a witness on the stand, and tell what I have perceived." The morning and the evening were sweet to me, and I led a life aloof from the society of men. I wondered if a mortal had ever known what I knew. I looked in books for some recognition of a kindred experience, but, strange to say, I found none. Indeed, I was slow to discover that other men had had this experience, for it had been possible to read books and to associate with men on other grounds. . . . I was daily intoxicated, and yet no man could call me intemperate. With all your science can you tell how it is, and whence it is, that light comes into the soul?

—JOU ii, 306–7

July 19, 1851

Here I am thirty-four years old, and yet my life is almost wholly unexpanded. How much is in the germ! There is such an interval between my ideal and the actual in many instances that I may say I am unborn. There is the instinct for society, but no society. Life is not long enough for one success. Within another thirty-four years that miracle can hardly take place. Methinks my seasons revolve more slowly than those of nature; I am differently timed. I am contented. This rapid revolution of nature, even of nature in me, why should it hurry me? Let a man step to the music which he hears, however measured. Is it important that I should mature as soon as an apple tree? Aye, as soon as an oak? May not my life in nature, in proportion as it is supernatural, be only the spring and infantile portion of my spirit's life? Shall I turn my spring to summer?. . . .

My spirit's unfolding observes not the pace of nature. The society which I was made for is not here. —JOU ii, 316–17

July 21, 1851

The forenoon is fuller of light. The butterflies on the flowers look like other and frequently larger flowers themselves. Now I yearn for one of those old, meandering, dry, uninhabited roads, which lead away from towns, which lead us away from temptation, which conduct to the outside of earth, over its uppermost crust. Where you may forget in what country you are traveling. . . . Where my spirit is free; where the walls and fences are not cared for; where your head is more in heaven than your feet are on earth . . . where it makes no odds which way you face, whether you are going or coming, whether it is morning or evening, mid-noon or midnight; where earth is cheap enough by being public; where you can walk and think with least obstruction, there being nothing to measure progress by; . . . by which you may go to the uttermost parts of the earth. It is wide enough, wide as the thoughts it allows to visit you. Sometimes it is some particular half-dozen rods which I wish to find myself pacing over, as where certain airs blow. Then my life will come to me, methinks; like a hunter I walk in wait for it. —JOU ii, 322–23

July 23, 1851

The mind is subject to moods as the shadows of clouds pass over the earth. Pay not too much heed to them. Let not the traveler stop for them. They consist with the fairest weather. By the mood of my mind I suddenly felt dissuaded from continuing my walk. But I observed at the same instant that the shadow of a cloud was passing over [the] spot on which I stood, though it was of small extent, which, if it had no connection with my mood, at any rate suggested how transient and little to be regarded that mood was. I kept on and in a moment the sun shone on my walk within and without.

—JOU ii, 340

August 5, 1851, 7:30 p.m.

Moon half full. I sit beside Hubbard's Grove. . . . It is 8 o'clock. The farmer has driven in his cows and is cutting an armful of green corn fodder for them. . . .

The mosquitoes hum about me. I distinguish the modest moonlight on my paper.

As the twilight deepens and the moonlight is more and more bright, I begin to distinguish myself, who I am and where. As my walls contract, I become more collected and composed and sensible of my own existence as when a lamp is brought into a dark apartment and I see who the company are. With a coolness and the mildest silvery light, I recover some sanity. My thoughts are more distinct, moderated, and tempered. Reflection is more possible while the day goes by. The intense light of the sun unfits me for meditation, makes me wander in my thought. My life is too diffuse and dissipated. Routine succeeds and prevails over us. The trivial has greater power then, and most at noon day, the most trivial hour of the twenty-four. I am sobered by the moonlight. I bethink myself. It is like a cup of cold water to a thirsty man. The moonlight is more favorable to meditation than sunlight.

The sun lights this world from without, shines in at a window, but the moon is like a lamp within an apartment. It shines for us. . . . The question is not what you look at, but how you see.

—JOU ii, 370–73

August 16, 1851

It is true [that] man can and does live by preying on other animals, but this is a miserable way of sustaining himself, and he will be regarded as a benefactor of his race, along with Prometheus and Christ, who shall teach men to live on a more innocent and wholesome diet. Is it not already acknowledged to be a reproach that man is a carnivorous animal? —JOU ii, 390

August 17, 1851

For a day or two it has been quite cool, a coolness that was felt even when sitting by an open window in a thin coat on the west side of the house in the morning, and you naturally sought the sun at that hour. . . . I feel as if this coolness would do me good. If it only makes my life more pensive! Why should pensiveness be akin to sadness? There is a certain fertile sadness which I would not avoid, but rather earnestly seek. It is positively joyful to me. It saves my life from being trivial. My life flows with a deeper current, no longer as a shallow and brawling stream, parched and shrunken by the summer heats. . . . My heart leaps into my mouth at the sound of the wind in the woods. I, whose life was but yesterday so desultory and shallow, suddenly recover my spirits, my spirituality, through my hearing. . . . Ah! If I could so live that there should be no desultory moment in all my life! That in the trivial season, when small fruits are ripe, my fruits might he ripe also! That I could match nature always with my moods! That in each season when some part of nature especially flourishes, then a corresponding part of me may not fail to flourish! Ah, I would walk, I would sit and sleep, with natural piety! What if I could pray aloud or to myself as I went along by the brooksides, a cheerful prayer like the birds . . . ! The quivering of pigeons' wings reminds me of the tough fiber of the air which they rend. I thank you God. I do not deserve anything. I am unworthy of the least regard; and yet I am made to rejoice. I am impure and worthless, and yet the world is gilded for my delight and holidays are prepared for me, and my path is strewn with flowers.

—JOU ii, 390–92

August 19, 1851

This is a world where there are flowers. Now at 5 a.m. the fog which in the west looks like a wreath of hard-rolled cotton batting is rapidly dispersing. . . . The grass is very wet with dew this morning. . . .

The poet must be continually watching the moods of his mind, as the astronomer watches the aspects of the heavens. What might we not expect from a long life faithfully spent in this wise? . . . As travelers go round the world and report natural objects and phenomena, so faithfully let another stay at home and report the phenomena of his own life—catalogue stars, those thoughts whose orbits are as rarely calculated as comets. It matters not whether they visit my mind or yours—whether the meteor falls in my field or in yours—only that it come from heaven. . . . A meteorological journal of the mind. You shall observe what occurs in your latitude, I in mine. . . .

Those who have no knowledge of the divine appoint themselves defenders of the divine, as champions of the church, etc. I have been astonished to observe how long some audiences can endure to hear a man speak on a subject which he knows nothing about, as religion for instance. . . .

I fear that the character of my knowledge is from year to year becoming more distinct and scientific; that, in exchange for views as wide as heaven's cope, I am being narrowed down to the field of the microscope. I see details, not wholes nor the shadow of the whole. —JOU ii, 401–6

August 21, 1851

The intellect of most men is barren. They neither fertilize nor are fertilized. It is the marriage of the soul with Nature that makes the intellect fruitful, that gives birth to imagination. —JOU ii, 413

September 7, 1851

Our ecstatic states, which appear to yield so little fruit, have this value at least: though in the seasons when our genius reigns, we may be powerless for expression, yet, in calmer seasons, when our talent is active, the memory of those rarer moods comes to color our picture and is the permanent paint pot, as it were, into which we dip our brush. . . . It is an experience of infinite beauty on which we unfailingly draw, which enables us to exaggerate ever truly. Our moments of inspiration are not lost though we have no particular poem to show for them; for those experiences have left an indelible impression, and we are ever and anon reminded of them. . . .

We are receiving our portion of the infinite. The art of life! Was there ever anything memorable written upon it? By what disciplines to secure the most life, with what care to watch our thoughts. To observe what transpires, not in the street, but in the mind and heart of me! I do not remember any page which will tell me how to spend this afternoon. I do not so much wish to know how to economize time as how to spend it, by what means to grow rich, that the day may not have been in vain.

[Natural] scenery, when it is truly seen, reacts on the life of the seer. How to live. How to get the most life. . . . How to extract its honey from the flower of the world. That is my everyday business. I am as busy as a bee about it. I ramble over all fields on that errand, and am never so happy as when I feel myself heavy with honey and wax. I am like a bee searching the livelong day for the sweets of nature. . . . The art of spending a day. If it is possible that we may be addressed, it behooves us to be attentive. If by watching all day and all night, I may detect some trace of the ineffable, then will it not be worth the while to watch? Watch and pray without ceasing, but not necessarily in sadness. Be of good cheer. . . .

I am convinced that men are not well employed, that this is not the way to spend a day. If by patience, if by watching, I can secure one new ray of light, can feel myself elevated for an instant, . . . the world which was dead prose to me become living and divine, shall I not watch ever? . . . We are surrounded by a rich and fertile mystery. May we not probe it, pry into it, employ ourselves about it, a little? To devote your life to the discovery of the divinity in nature, or to the eating of oysters, would they not be attended with very different results? . . .

To watch for, describe, all the divine features which I detect in Nature.

My profession is to be always on the alert to find God in nature, to know his lurking-places, to attend all the oratorios, the operas, in nature. —JOU ii, 468–72

October 14, 1851

Some men's lives are but an aspiration, a yearning toward a higher state, and they are wholly misapprehended, until they are referred to, or traced through, all their metamorphoses. We cannot pronounce upon a man's intellectual and moral state until we foresee what metamorphosis it is preparing him for. —JOU iii, 71

November 13, 1851

A cold and dark afternoon, the sun being behind clouds in the west. The landscape is barren of objects, the trees being leafless, and so little light in the sky for variety. . . . Now is the time to cut timber for yokes and ox-bows, leaving the tough bark on—yokes for your own neck. Finding yourself yoked to Matter and to Time. Truly a hard day, hard times these! Not a mosquito left. Not an insect to hum. Crickets gone into winter quarters. Friends long since gone there, and you left to walk on frozen ground, with your hands in your pockets. Ah, but is not this a glorious time for your deep inward fires? . . . All fields lie fallow. Shall not your mind? True, the freezing ground is being prepared for immeasurable snows, but there are brave thoughts within you that shall remain to rustle the winter through like white oak leaves upon your boughs. —JOU iii, 110–11

November 16, 1851

So far as thinking is concerned, surely original thinking is the divinest thing. . . . We check and repress the divinity that stirs within us, to fall down and worship the divinity that is dead without us. —JOU iii, 119

December 12, 1851

Ah, dear nature, the mere remembrance, after a short forgetfulness, of the pine woods! I come to it as a hungry man to a crust of bread.

I have been surveying for twenty or thirty days, living coarsely, even as respects my diet, for I find that that will always alter to suit my employment—indeed, leading a quite trivial life; and tonight, for the first time, had made a fire in my chamber and endeavored to return to myself. I wished to ally myself to the powers that rule the universe. I wished to dive into some deep stream of thoughtful and devoted life, which meandered through retired and fertile meadows far from towns. I wished to do again, or for once, things quite congenial to my highest, inmost, and most sacred nature, to lurk in crystalline thought like the trout under verdurous banks, where stray mankind should only see my bubble come to the surface. I wished to live, ah! as far away as a man can think. I wished for leisure and quiet to let my life flow in its proper channels, with its proper currents. —JOU iii, 133

December 25, 1851

I go forth to see the sun set. Who knows how it will set, even half an hour beforehand? Whether it will go down in clouds or a clear sky? . . .

I witness a beauty in the form or coloring of the clouds which addresses itself to my imagination, for which you account scientifically to my understanding, but do not so account to my imagination. It is what it suggests and is the symbol of that I care for, and if, by any trick of science, you rob it of its symbolicalness, you do me no service and explain nothing. I, standing twenty miles off, see a crimson cloud in the horizon. . . .

You tell me it is a mass of vapor which absorbs all other rays and reflects the red, but that is nothing to the purpose, for this red vision excites me, stirs my blood, makes my thoughts flow, and I have new and indescribable fancies, and you have not touched the secret of that influence. If there is not something mystical in your explanation, something unexplainable to the understanding, some elements of mystery, it is quite insufficient. If there is nothing in it which speaks to my imagination, what boots it? What sort of science is that which enriches the understanding, but robs the imagination? . . .

We seek too soon to ally the perceptions of the mind to the experience of the hand, to prove our gossamer truths practical, to show their connection with our everyday life (better show their distance from our everyday life), to relate them to the cider mill and the banking institution. Ah, give me pure mind, pure thought! . . . Perchance it may convince such that there are more things in heaven and earth than are dreamed of in their philosophy.

—JOU iii, 155–57

THE DEEPS OF SILENCE
1852–1862

In 1852, Thoreau began a study of the natural history of Concord. He traveled again to Maine on a difficult three-hundred mile canoe trek *and, in 1854, published* Walden. *He continued to lecture occasionally but could not establish himself as a regular presence on the lecture circuit as Emerson had. In the spring of 1855 Thoreau was struck with an illness that drained the strength from his legs and recurred periodically for the next two years. He went to New Jersey for a surveying job in 1856 and visited Walt Whitman in New York City. In July 1857 he returned for a final visit to the Maine woods and in 1858 explored the White Mountains in New Hampshire. When his father died in 1859, Thoreau became the head of the household and managed the family's pencil-manufacturing business. In 1860, he published his essay on "The Succession of Trees" in the* New York Tribune, *a study that established his reputation as a naturalist. In December Thoreau contracted a severe case of bronchitis, which would make him housebound through the winter and spring. In the summer of 1861 he traveled to Minnesota, hoping to regain his health but returned to Concord in worse condition than when he left.*

Understanding his illness to be fatal, and though bedridden, Thoreau used his remaining months to prepare his essays for publication. He died on May 6, 1862, at the age of forty-four.

June 22, 1852

We have had a succession of thunder showers today and at sunset a rainbow. How moral the world is made! This bow is not utilitarian. Methinks men are great in proportion as they are moral! . . . Is not the rainbow a faint vision of God's face? How glorious should be the life of man passed under this arch! What more remarkable phenomenon than a rainbow, yet how little it is remarked! —JOU iv, 128

August 8, 1852

The entertaining [of] a single thought of a certain elevation makes all men of one religion. It is always some base alloy that creates the distinction of sects. Thought greets thought over the widest gulfs of time . . . I know, for instance, that Sadi [thirteenth-century Sufi poet] entertained once identically the same thought that I do, and therefore I can find no essential difference between Sadi and myself. He is not Persian, he is not ancient, he is not strange to me. By the identity of his thoughts with mine he still survives. . . . In his thought I have a sample of him, a slice from his core, which makes it unimportant where certain bones which the thinker once employed may lie; but I could not have got this without being equally entitled to it with himself. —JOU iv, 289–90

September 1852

Mr. Blake—

All transcendent goodness is one, though appreciated in different ways, or by different senses. In beauty we see it, in music we hear it, in fragrance we scent it, in the palatable the pure palate tastes it, and in rare health the whole body feels it. . . . The lover sees in the glance of his beloved the same beauty that in the sunset paints the western skies. It is the same daimon. . . .

—Letter to Harrison Blake, LSS, 69

February 27, 1853

Mr. Blake—

I have not answered your letter before because I have been almost constantly in the fields surveying of late. It is long since I have spent so many days so profitably in a pecuniary sense; so unprofitably, it seems to me, in a more important sense. . . .

As to whether what you speak of as the "world's way" (which for the most part is my way) or that which is shown me, is the better, the former is imposture, the latter is truth. . . . The one is the way of death, the other of life everlasting. . . .

I have had but one *spiritual* birth (excuse the word), and now whether it rains or snows, whether I laugh or cry, fall farther below, or approach nearer to my standard . . . not a new scintillation of light flashes on me, but ever and anon, though with longer intervals, the same surprising and everlastingly new light dawns to me. . . .

The problem of life becomes one cannot say by how many more degrees complicated as our material wealth is increased . . . since the problem is not merely nor mainly to get life for our bodies, but by this or a similar discipline to get life for our souls. . . .

—Letter to Harrison Blake, LSS, 81–84

March 5, 1853

The secretary of the Association for the Advancement of Science requests me, as he probably has thousands of others, by a printed circular letter from Washington the other day, to fill the blank against certain questions, among which the most important one was what branch of science I was specially interested in. . . . I felt that it would be to make myself the laughingstock of the scientific community to describe or attempt to describe to them that branch of science which specially interests me, inasmuch as they do not believe in a science which deals with the higher law. . . . The fact is I am a mystic, a transcendentalist, and a natural philosopher to boot. Now I think of it, I should have told them at once that I was a transcendentalist. That would have been the shortest way of telling them that they would not understand my explanations.

How absurd that, though I probably stand as near to nature as any of them, and am by constitution as good an observer as most, yet a true account of my relation to nature should excite their ridicule only! If it had been the secretary of an association of which Plato or Aristotle was the president, I should not have hesitated to describe my studies at once and particularly.

—JOU v, 4–5

April 10, 1853

Mr. Blake—

Of what use were it, pray, to get a little wood to burn, to warm your body this cold weather, if there were not a divine fire kindled at the same time to warm your spirit? . . . I cuddle up by my stove, and there I get up another fire which warms fire itself. Life is so short that it is not wise to take roundabout ways, nor can we spend much time in waiting. —Letter to Harrison Blake, LSS, 91

December 19 and 22, 1853

Mr. Blake—

My debt has accumulated so that I should have answered your letter at once, if I had not been the subject of what is called a press of engagements, having a lecture to write for last Wednesday. . . .

You speak of doing and being, and the vanity, real or apparent, of much doing. . . .

You say that you do not succeed much. Does it concern you enough that you do not? Do you work hard enough at it? Do you get the benefit of discipline out of it? If so, persevere. . . .

If you are going into that line—going to besiege the city of God—you must not only be strong in engines, but prepared with provisions to starve out the garrison. . . .

Whether a man spends his day in an ecstasy or despondency, he must do some work to show for it, even as there are flesh and bones to show for him. We are superior to the joy we experience. . . . —Letter to Harrison Blake, LSS, 93–97

May 10, 1853

It is remarkable that I saw this morning for the first time the bobolink, gold robin, and kingbird—and have since heard the first two in various parts of the town and am satisfied that they have just come—and, in the woods, the veery [a songbird] note. I hear the ringing sound of the toads borne on the rippling wind as I keep down the causeway.

He is the richest who has most use for nature as raw material of tropes and symbols with which to describe his life. If these gates of golden willows affect me, they correspond to the beauty and promise of some experience on which I am entering. If I am overflowing with life, am rich in experience for which I lack expression, then nature will be my language full of poetry—all nature will *fable*, and every natural phenomenon be a myth. The man of science, who is not seeking for expression but for a fact to be expressed merely, studies nature as a dead language. I pray for such inward experience as will make nature significant.

—JOU v, 135

October 26, 1853

How watchful we must be to keep the crystal well that we were made, clear!—that it be not made turbid by our contact with the world, so that it will not reflect objects. What other liberty is there worth having, if we have not freedom and peace in our minds, if our inmost and most private man is but a sour and turbid pool? Often we are so jarred by chagrins in dealing with the world that we cannot reflect. Everything beautiful impresses us as sufficient to itself. . . .

Ah! The world is too much with us, and our whole soul is stained by what it works in, like the dyer's hand. A man had better starve at once than lose his innocence in the process of getting his bread.

—JOU v, 453–54

December 22, 1853

I have offered myself much more earnestly as a lecturer than a surveyor. Yet I do not get any employment as a lecturer. . . . But they who do not make the highest demand on you shall rue it. It is because they make a low demand on themselves. . . . Woe be to the generation that lets any higher faculty in its midst go unemployed! That is to deny God and know him not, and he, accordingly, will know not of them. —JOU vi, 21–22

January 21, 1854

Mr. Blake—

I am glad to hear that I do not always limit your vision when you look this way—that you sometimes see the light through me, that I am here and there windows and not all dead wall. . . .

—Letter to Harrison Blake, LSS, 101–2

May 6, 1854

The man of most science is the man most alive, whose life is the greatest event. Senses that take cognizance of outward things merely are of no avail. It matters not where or how far you travel—the farther commonly the worse—but how much alive you are. If it is possible to conceive of an event outside to [sic] humanity, it is not of the slightest significance, though it were the explosion of a planet. . . . No mere willful activity whatever, whether in writing verses or collecting statistics, will produce true poetry or science. If you are really a sick man, it is indeed to be regretted, for you cannot accomplish so much as if you were well. All that a man has to say or do that can possibly concern mankind, is in some shape or other to tell the story of his love—to sing; and, if he is fortunate and keeps alive, he will be forever in love. —JOU vi, 237

June 16, 1854

Again I scent the white water lily, and a season I had waited for is arrived. How indispensable [are] all these experiences to make up the summer! It is the emblem of purity and its scent suggests it. Growing in stagnant and muddy water, it bursts up so pure and fair to the eye and so sweet to the scent, as if to show us what purity, and sweetness reside in, and can be extracted from, the slime and muck of earth. I think I have plucked the first one that is opened for a mile at least. What confirmation of our hopes is in the fragrance of the water lily! I shall not so soon despair of the world for it, notwithstanding slavery, and the cowardice and want of principle of the North. It suggests that the time may come when man's deeds will smell as sweet. Such, then, is the odor our planet emits. Who can doubt, then, that Nature is young and sound? If Nature can compound this fragrance still annually, I shall believe her still full of vigor, and that there is virtue in man, too, who perceives and loves it. It is as if all the pure and sweet and virtuous was extracted from the slime and decay of earth and presented thus in a flower. The resurrection of virtue! . . . This fragrance assures me that though all other men fall, one shall stand fast; though a pestilence sweep over the earth, it shall at least spare one man. The genius of Nature is unimpaired. Her flowers are as fair and as fragrant as ever.

—JOU vi, 352–53

August 2, 1854

I feel the necessity of deepening the stream of my life; I must cultivate privacy. It is very dissipating to be with people too much. . . . I cannot spare my moonlight and my mountains for the best of man I am likely to get in exchange.

I am inclined now for a pensive evening walk. . . .

As I go up the hill, surrounded by its shadow, while the sun is setting, I am soothed by the delicious stillness of the evening, save that on the hills the wind blows. I was surprised by the sound of my own voice. It is an atmosphere burdensome with thought. For the first time for a month, at least, I am reminded that thought is possible. The din of trivialness is silenced. I float over or through the deeps of silence. It is the first silence I have heard for a month. My life had been a River Platte, tinkling over its sands but useless for all great navigation, but now it suddenly became a fathomless ocean. It shelved off to unimagined depths.

—JOU vi, 416–17

September 9, 1854

This morning I find a little hole, three quarters of an inch or an inch over, above my small tortoise eggs, and find a young tortoise coming out. . . . I buried them in the garden June fifteenth.

I am affected by the thought that the earth nurses these eggs. They are planted in the earth, and the earth takes care of them; she is genial to them and does not kill them. It suggests a certain vitality and intelligence in the earth, which I had not realized. This mother is not merely inanimate and inorganic. Though the immediate mother turtle abandons her offspring, the earth and sun are kind to them. The old turtle on which the earth rests takes care of them while the other waddles off. . . . The earth has some virtue in it; when seeds are put into it, they germinate; when turtles' eggs, they hatch in due time. Though the mother turtle remained and brooded them, it would still nevertheless be the universal world turtle which, through her, cared for them as now. Thus the earth is the mother of all creatures.

—JOU vii, 28–29

December 6, 1854

After lecturing twice this winter, I feel that I am in danger of cheapening myself by trying to become a successful lecturer, *i.e.*, to interest my audiences. I am disappointed to find that the most that I am and value myself for is lost, or worse than lost, on my audience. I fail to get even the attention of the mass. I should suit them better if I suited myself less. I feel that the public demand an average man—average thoughts and manners—not originality, not even absolute excellence. You cannot interest them except as you are like them and sympathize with them. I would rather that my audience come to me then that I should go to them, and so they be sifted—*i.e.*, I would rather write books than lectures. . . . To read to a promiscuous audience who are at your mercy, the fine thoughts you solaced yourself with far away, is as violent as to fatten geese by cramming, and in this case they do not get fatter.

—JOU vii, 79–80

June 11, 1855

When I would go a-visiting, I find that I go off the fashionable street—not being inclined to change my dress—to where man meets man and not polished shoe meets shoe. . . .

What if we feel a yearning to which no breast answers? I walk alone. My heart is full. Feelings impede the current of my thoughts. I knock on the earth for my friend. I expect to meet him at every turn, but no friend appears, and perhaps none is dreaming of me. I am tired of frivolous society, in which silence is forever the most natural and the best manners. I would fain walk on the deep waters, but my companions will only walk on shallows and puddles. I am naturally silent in the midst of twenty from day to day, from year to year. . . . One talks to me of his apples and pears, and I depart with my secret untold. His are not the apples that tempt me. —JOU vii, 416–17

September 26, 1855

Mr. Blake—

To what end do I lead a simple life at all, pray? That I may teach others to simplify their lives?—and so all our lives be *simplified* merely, like an algebraic formula? Or not, rather, that I make use of the ground I have cleared, to live more worthily and profitably? I would fain lay the most stress forever on that which is the most important—imports the most to me—though it were only . . . a vibration in the air. As a preacher, I should be prompted to tell men, not so much how to get their wheat bread cheaper, as of the bread of life compared with which *that* is bran. . . .

But how do *you* do? . . . Do you find anything in which you can work, accomplishing something solid from day to day? Have you put sloth and doubt behind, considerably?

—Letter to Harrison Blake, LSS, 125–26

October 18, 1855

Last night I was reading [Alfred William] Howitt's account of the Australian gold diggings, and had in my mind's eye the numerous valleys with their streams all cut up with foul pits, ten to one hundred feet deep, and half a dozen feet across, as close as they can be dug, and half full of water, where men furiously rush to probe for their fortunes, . . . turned into demons and regardless of each other's rights in their thirst after riches, whole valleys for thirty miles suddenly honeycombed by the pits of the miners, so that hundreds are drowned in them. . . . I asked myself why I might not be washing some gold daily, though it were only the finest particles, or might not sink the shaft down to the gold within me and work that mine. . . . Pursue some path, however narrow and crooked, in which you can walk with love and reverence. Wherever a man separates from the multitude and goes his own way, there is a fork in the road, though the travelers along the highway see only a gap in the paling. —JOU vii, 491–92

December 11, 1855

For the first time I wear gloves, but I have not walked *early* this season. . . .

I am reminded of the incredible phenomenon of small birds in winter, that ere long, amid the cold powdery snow, as it were a fruit of the season, will come twittering a flock of delicate crimson-tinged birds, lesser redpolls, to sport and feed on the seeds and buds now just right for them on the sunny side of the wood, shaking down the powdery snow there in their cheerful social feeding, as if it were high midsummer to them. . . . What a rich contrast! tropical colors, crimson breasts, on cold white snow! . . . The snow will be three feet deep, the ice will be two feet thick, and last night, perchance, the mercury sank to thirty degrees below zero. All the fountains of nature seem to be sealed up. The traveler is frozen on his way. But under the edge of yonder birch wood will be a little flock of crimson-breasted lesser redpolls, busily feeding on the seeds of the birch and shaking down the powdery snow! . . .

My body is all sentient. As I go here or there, I am tickled by this or that I come in contact with, as if I touched the wires of a battery. . . . The age of miracles is each moment thus returned.

Now it is wild apples, now river reflections, now a flock of lesser redpolls. In winter too, resides immortal youth and perennial summer.

—JOU viii, 41–44

April 9, 1856

The communications from the gods to us are still deep and sweet, indeed, but scanty and transient—enough only to keep alive the memory of the past.

—JOU viii, 269

August 30, 1856

Many of our days should be spent, not in vain expectations and lying on our oars, but in carrying out deliberately and faithfully the hundred little purposes which every man's genius must have suggested to him. Let not your life be wholly without an object, though it be only to ascertain the flavor of a cranberry, for it will not be only the quality of an insignificant berry that you will have tasted, but the flavor of your life to that extent, and it will be such a sauce as no wealth can buy. . . .

I have got in my huckleberries. I shall be ready for Thanksgiving. It is in vain to dream of a wildness distant from ourselves. There is none such. It is the bog in our brain and bowels, the primitive vigor of Nature in us, that inspires that dream. I shall never find in the wilds of Labrador any greater wildness than in some recess in Concord, *i.e.,* than I import into it. A little more manhood or virtue will make the surface of the globe anywhere thrillingly novel and wild. . . .

I see that all is not garden and cultivated fields and crops, that there are square rods in Middlesex County as purely primitive and wild as they were a thousand years ago, which have escaped the plow and the axe and the scythe and the cranberry rake, little oases of wildness in the desert of our civilization, wild as a square rod on the moon, supposing it to be uninhabited. . . .

—JOU ix, 37–44

October 5, 1856

It is well to find your employment and amusement in simple and homely things. These wear best and yield most. I think I would rather watch the motions of these cows in their pasture for a day which I now see all headed one way and slowly advancing . . . than wander to Europe or Asia, . . . for it is only ourselves that we report in either case, and perchance we shall report a more restless and worthless self in the latter case than in the first.

—JOU ix, 104

January 4, 1857

After spending four or five days surveying and drawing a plan incessantly, I especially feel the necessity of putting myself in communication with nature again, to recover my tone, to withdraw out of the wearying and unprofitable world of affairs. The things I have been doing have but a fleeting and accidental importance, however much men are immersed in them, and yield very little valuable fruit. I would fain have been wading through the woods and fields and conversing with the sane snow.

Having waded in the very shallowest stream of time, I would now bathe my temples in eternity. I wish again to participate in the serenity of nature, to share the happiness of the river and the woods. I thus from time to time break off my connection with eternal truths and go with a shallow stream of human affairs, grinding at the mill of the Philistines; but when my task is done, with never-failing confidence, I devote myself to the infinite again. It would be sweet to deal with men more, I can imagine, but where dwell they? Not in the fields which I traverse.

—JOU ix, 205

January 7, 1857

I go through the woods toward the cliffs along the side of the Well Meadow Field.

There is nothing so sanative, so poetic, as a walk in the woods and fields even now, when I meet none abroad for pleasure. Nothing so inspires me and excites such serene and profitable thought. . . . But alone in distant woods or fields, in unpretending sprout-lands or pastures tracked by rabbits, even in a bleak and, to most, cheerless day, like this, when a villager would be thinking of his inn, I come to myself, I once more feel myself grandly related, and that cold and solitude are friends of mine. I suppose that this value, in my case, is equivalent to what others get by churchgoing and prayer. I come to my solitary woodland walk as the homesick go home. I thus dispose of the superfluous and see things as they are, grand and beautiful. . . . I come out to these solitudes, where the problem of existence is simplified. I get away a mile or two from the town into the stillness and solitude of nature, with rocks, trees, weeds, snow about me. I enter some glade in the woods, perchance, where a few weeds and dry leaves alone lift themselves above the surface of the snow, and it is as if I had come to an open window. I see out and around myself. . . . This is what I go out to seek. It is as if I always met in those places some grand, serene, immortal, infinitely encouraging, though invisible, companion, and I walked with him. There at last my nerves are steadied, my senses and my mind do their office. . . .

—JOU ix, 208–9

January 11, 1857

For some years past I have partially offered myself as a lecturer; have been advertised as such several years. Yet I have had but two or three invitations to lecture in a year, and some years none at all. I congratulate myself on having been permitted to stay at home thus, I am so much richer for it. I do not see what I should have got of much value, but money, by going about, but I do see what I should have lost. It seems to me that I have a longer and more liberal lease of life thus. I cannot afford to be telling my experience, especially to those who perhaps will take no interest in it. . . . As for the lecture-goers, it is none of their business what I think.

—JOU ix, 214–15

January 13, 1857

I hear one thrumming a guitar below stairs. It reminds me of moments that I have lived. What a comment on our life is the least strain of music! It lifts me up above all the dust and mire of the universe. I soar or hover with clean skirts over the field of my life. It is ever life within life, in concentric spheres. The field wherein I toil or rust at any time is at the same time the field for such different kinds of life! . . . The identical field where I am leading my humdrum life, let but a strain of music be heard there, is seen to be the field of some unrecorded crusade or tournament the thought of which excites in us an ecstasy of joy. The way in which I am affected by this faint thrumming advertises me that there is still some health and immortality in the springs of me. What an elixir is this sound! . . . It releases me; it bursts my bonds. Almost all, perhaps all, our life is, speaking comparatively, a stereotyped despair; i.e., we never at any time realize the full grandeur of our destiny. We forever and ever and habitually underrate our fate. Talk of infidels! Why, all of the race of man, except in the rarest moments when they are lifted above themselves by an ecstasy, are infidels. With the very best disposition, what does my belief amount to? This poor, timid, unenlightened, thick-skinned creature, what *can* it believe? I am, of course, hopelessly ignorant and unbelieving until some divinity stirs within me. Ninety-nine one-hundredths of our lives we are mere hedgers and ditchers, but from time to time we meet with reminders of our destiny.

We hear the kindred vibrations, music! and we put out our dormant feelers unto the limits of the universe. We attain to a wisdom that passeth understanding. —JOU ix, 217–18

May 12, 1857

While dropping beans in the garden at Texas [the Thoreau home] just after sundown, . . . I hear from across the fields the note of the bay-wing, *Come here here there there quick quick quick or I'm gone* (which I have no doubt sits on some fence post or rail there), and it instantly translates me from the sphere of my work and repairs all the world that we jointly inhabit. It reminds me of so many country afternoons and evenings when this bird's strain was heard far over the fields, as I pursued it from field to field. The spirit of its earth song, of its serene and true philosophy, was breathed into me, and I saw the world as through a glass, as it lies eternally. Some of its aboriginal contentment, even of its domestic felicity, possessed me. What he suggests is permanently true. As the bay-wing sang many a thousand years ago, so sang he tonight. In the beginning God heard his song and pronounced it good, and hence it has endured. . . .

I ordinarily plod along a sort of whitewashed prison entry, subject to some indifferent or even groveling mood. . . . I take incredibly narrow views, live on the limits, and have no recollection of absolute truth. Mushroom institutions hedge me in. But suddenly, in some fortunate moment, the voice of eternal wisdom reaches me even, in the strain of the sparrow, and liberates me, whets and clarifies my senses, makes me a competent witness.

—JOU ix, 363–65

July 2, 1857

Calla palustris . . . at the south end of Gowing's Swamp. Having found this in one place, I now find it in another. Many an object is not seen, though it falls within the range of our visual ray, because . . . we are not looking for it. So, in the largest sense, we find only the world we look for. —JOU ix, 466

November 18, 1857

Prevailing sights and sounds make the impression of beauty and music on me. But in sickness all is deranged. I had yesterday a kink in my back and a general cold, and as usual it amounted to a cessation of life. I lost with the time my *rapport* or relation to nature. Sympathy with nature is an evidence of perfect health. You cannot perceive beauty but with a serene mind. The cheaper your amusements, the safer and saner. . . . Each man's necessary path, though as obscure and apparently uneventful as that of a beetle in the grass, is the way to the deepest joys he is susceptible of. Though he converses only with moles and fungi and disgraces his relatives, it is no matter if he knows what is steel to his flint.

—JOU x, 188

January 6, 1858

The first snowstorm of much importance. By noon it may be six inches deep. . . .

I was feeling very cheap, nevertheless, reduced to make the most of dry dogwood berries. Very little evidence of God or man did I see just then, and life not as rich and inviting an enterprise as it should be, when my attention was caught by a snowflake on my coat sleeve. It was one of those perfect, crystalline, star-shaped ones, six rayed, like a flat wheel with six spokes. . . . This little object, which, with many of its fellows, rested unmelting on my coat, so perfect and beautiful, reminded me that Nature had not lost her pristine vigor yet, and why should man lose heart? . . . I confess that I was a little encouraged, for I was beginning to believe that Nature was poor and mean, and I was now convinced that she turned off as good work as ever. What a world we live in! Where are the jewelers' shops? There is nothing handsomer than a snowflake and a dewdrop. I may say that the maker of the world exhausts his skill with each snowflake and dewdrop that he sends down. We think that the one mechanically coheres and that the other simply flows together and falls, but in truth they are the product of *enthusiasm*, the children of an ecstasy, finished with the artist's utmost skill. —JOU x, 238–40

May 6, 1858

The thinker, he who is serene and self-possessed, is the brave, not the desperate soldier. He who can deal with his thoughts as a material, building them into poems in which future generations will delight, he is the man of the greatest and rarest vigor, not sturdy diggers and lusty polygamists. He is a man of energy, in whom settled and poetic thoughts are bred. . . . There is no more Herculean task than to think a thought about this life and then get it expressed. —JOU x, 404–5

August 18, 1858

What is religion? That which is never spoken. —JOU, xi, 113

November 1, 1858

As the afternoons grow shorter, and the early evening drives us home to complete our chores, we are reminded of the shortness of life, and become more pensive, at least in this twilight of the year. . . . I leaned over a rail in the twilight on the Walden Road, waiting for the evening mail to be distributed, when such thoughts visited me. I seemed to recognize the November evening as a familiar thing come round again, and yet I could hardly tell whether I had ever known it or only divined it. . . . It was as if I was promised the greatest novelty the world has ever seen or shall see, though the utmost possible novelty would be the difference between me and myself a year ago. This alone encouraged me, and was my fuel for the approaching winter. That we may behold the panorama with this slight improvement or change, this is what we sustain life for with so much effort from year to year.

And yet there is no more tempting novelty then this new November. No going to Europe or another world is to be named with it. Give me the old familiar walk, post office and all, with this ever new self, with this infant expectation and faith, which does not know when it is beaten. We'll go nutting once more. We'll pluck the nut of the world, and crack it in the winter evenings. Theaters and all other sightseeing are puppet shows in comparison. I will take another walk to the cliff, another row on the river, another skate on the meadow, be out in the first snow, associate with the winter birds. Here I am at home. In the bare and bleached crust of the earth I recognize my friend. . . .

Here, of course, is all that you love, all that you expect, all that you are. Here is your bride elect, as close to you as she can be got. Here is all the best and all the worst you can imagine. What more do you want? . . . Foolish people imagine that what they imagine is somewhere else. That stuff is not made in any factory but their own.

—JOU xi, 273–75

November 4, 1858

If, about the last of October, you ascend any hill in the outskirts of the town and look over the forest, you will see, amid the brown of other oaks, which are now withered, and the green of the pines, the bright red tops or crescents of the scarlet oaks, very equally and thickly distributed on all sides, even to the horizon. . . . All this you will see, and much more, if you are prepared to see it—if you *look* for it. . . . Objects are concealed from our view not so much because they are out of the course of our visual ray, as because there is no intention of the mind and eye toward them. We do not realize how far and widely, or how near and narrowly, we are to look. The greater part of the phenomena of nature are for this reason concealed to us all our lives. . . . Nature does not cast pearls before swine. There is just as much beauty visible to us in the landscape as we are prepared to appreciate—not a grain more. . . . The scarlet oak must, in a sense, be in your eye when you go forth. We cannot see anything until we are possessed with the idea of it, and then we can hardly see anything else. —JOU xi, 284–85

November 30, 1858

I cannot but see still in my mind's eye those little striped bream [a freshwater fish] poised in Walden's glaucous water. They balance all the rest of the world in my estimation at present, for this is the bream that I have just found. . . . It is not like a new bird, a transient visitor that may not be seen again for years, but there it dwells and has dwelt permanently, who can tell how long? . . . But in my account of this bream, I cannot go a hair's breadth beyond the mere statement that it exists—the miracle of its existence, my contemporary and neighbor, yet so different from me! I can only poise my thought there by its side and try to think like a bream for a moment. I can only think of precious jewels, of music, poetry, beauty, and the mystery of life. I only see the bream in its orbit, as I see a star, but I care not to measure its distance or weight. The bream, appreciated, floats in the pond as the center of the system, another image of God. Its life no man can explain more than he can his own. —JOU xi, 258–59

January 2, 1859

Going up the hill through Stow's young oak woodland, I listen to the sharp, dry rustle of the withered oak leaves. This is the voice of the wood now. . . . It rises and falls, wells and dies away, with agreeable alternation as the sea surf does. Perhaps the landsman can foretell a storm by it. It is remarkable how universal these grand murmurs are, these backgrounds of sound—the surf, the wind in the forest, waterfalls, etc.—which yet to the ear and in their origin are essentially one voice, the earth voice, the breathing or snoring of the creature. The earth is our ship, and this is the sound of the wind in her rigging as we sail. —JOU xi, 384

February 5, 1859

When we have experienced many disappointments, such as the loss of friends, the notes of birds ceased to affect us as they did. —JOU xi, 439

February 25, 1859

Measure your health by your sympathy with morning and the spring. If there is no response in you to the awakening of nature—if the prospect of an early morning walk does not banish sleep, if the warble of the first bluebird does not thrill you—know that the morning and spring of your life are past. Thus may you feel your pulse. —JOU xi, 455

April 24, 1859

Nothing must be postponed. Take time by the forelock. Now or never! You must live in the present, launch yourself on every wave, find your eternity in each moment. . . . Let us see vessels sailing prosperously before the wind, and not simply stranded barks. There is no world for the penitent and regretful. —JOU xii, 159–60

October 4, 1859

It is only when we forget all our learning that we begin to know. I do not get nearer by a hair's breadth to any natural object so long as I presume that I have an introduction to it from some learned man. To conceive of it with a total apprehension I must for the thousandth time approach it as something totally strange. If you would make acquaintance with the ferns you must forget your botany. You must get rid of what is commonly called *knowledge* of them. Not a single scientific term or distinction is the least to the purpose, for you would fain perceive something, and you must approach the object totally unprejudiced. You must be aware that *no thing* is what you have taken it to be. In what book is this world and its beauty described? Who has plotted the steps toward the discovery of beauty? You have got to be in a different state from common. Your greatest success will be simply to perceive that such things are. . . . —JOU xii, 371

October 15, 1859

Each town should have a park, or rather a primitive forest, of five hundred or a thousand acres, where a stick should never be cut for fuel, a common possession forever, for instruction and recreation. We hear of cow commons and ministerial lots [set aside for the town's minister], but we want *men*-commons and lay lots, inalienable forever. Let us keep the New World *new*, preserve all the advantages of living in the country. . . . All Walden Wood might have been preserved for our park forever, with Walden [Pond] in its midst and the Easterbrooks country, an unoccupied area of some four square miles might have been our huckleberry field. If any owners of these tracts are about to leave the world without natural heirs who need or deserve to be especially remembered, they will do wisely to abandon their possession to all, and not will them to some individual who perhaps has enough already. —JOU xii, 387

October 18, 1859

Why can we not oftener refresh one another with original thoughts? If the fragrance of the dicksonia fern is so grateful and suggestive to us, how much more refreshing and encouraging—re-creating—would be fresh and fragrant thoughts communicated to us fresh from a man's experience and life! I want none of his pity, nor sympathy, in the common sense, but that he should emit and communicate to me his essential fragrance, that he should not be forever repenting and going to church (when not otherwise sinning), but, as it were, going a-huckleberrying in the fields of thought, and enrich all the world with his visions and his joys. —JOU xii, 399–400

January 27, 1860

Up river to Fair Haven Pond and return by Walden.

Half a dozen redpolls busily picking the seeds out of the larch cones behind Monroe's. . . .

When you think that your walk is profitless and a failure, and you can hardly persuade yourself not to return, it is on the point of being a success, for then you are in that subdued and knocking mood to which Nature never fails to open. —JOU xiii, 108–11

November 22, 1860

It is glorious to consider how independent man is of all enervating luxuries; and the poorer he is in respect to them, the richer he is. Summer is gone with all its infinite wealth, and still nature is genial to man. Though he no longer bathes in the stream, or reclines on the bank, or plucks berries on the hills, still he beholds the same inaccessible beauty around him. What though he has no juice of the grape stored up for him in cellars; the air itself is wine of an older vintage, and far more sanely exhilarating than any cellar affords. —JOU xiv, 259

November 25, 1860

How often you make a man richer in spirit in proportion as you rob him of earthly luxuries and comforts! —JOU xiv, 268

December 4, 1860

Talk about slavery! It is not the peculiar institution of the South. It exists wherever men are bought and sold, wherever a man allows himself to be made a mere thing or a tool, and surrenders his inalienable rights of reason and conscience. Indeed, this slavery is more complete than that which enslaves the body alone.

—JOU xiv, 292

January 3, 1861

The third considerable snowstorm. . . .

How few ever get beyond feeding, clothing, sheltering, and warming themselves in this world, and begin to treat themselves as human beings—as intellectual and moral beings! Most seem not to see any further, not to see over the ridge pole of their barns, or to be exhausted and accomplish nothing more than a full barn, though it may be accompanied by an empty head. . . .

But most men, it seems to me, do not care for Nature and would sell their share in all her beauty, as long as they may live, for a stated sum—many for a glass of rum. Thank God, men cannot as yet fly, and lay waste the sky as well as the earth! We are safe on that side for the present. —JOU xiv, 303–7

2

Essentials

Throughout his life Thoreau was determined to live a life stripped of superficiality and distraction, in order that he might fix his attention on "the essential facts of life" in his pursuit of the Actual. Much of his criticism of mid-nineteenth century American life was its unexamined emphasis on the material and institutional at the expense of the ideal and the idiosyncratic. He consciously minimized his physical needs to free himself for his "higher" pursuits and advocated and practiced the simple life with an almost religious fervor—"Simplify! Simplify! Simplify!"

HIGHER LAWS

We must learn to reawaken and keep ourselves awake, not by mechanical aids, but by an infinite expectation of the dawn, which does not forsake us in our soundest sleep. I know of no more encouraging fact than the unquestionable ability of man to elevate his life by a conscious endeavor. It is something to be able to paint a particular picture, or to carve a statue, and so to make a few objects beautiful; but it is far more glorious to carve and paint the very atmosphere and medium through which we look, which morally we can do. To affect the quality of the day, that is the highest of arts. Every man is tasked to make his life, even in its details, worthy of the contemplation of his most elevated and critical hour. —WAL, 85

Let us spend one day as deliberately as Nature, and not be thrown off the track by every nutshell and mosquito's wing that falls on the rails. Let us rise early and fast, or break fast, gently and without perturbation; let company come and let company go, let the bells ring and the children cry—determined to make a day of it. Why should we knock under and go with the stream?. . . . Let us settle ourselves, and work and wedge our feet downward through the mud and slush of opinion, and prejudice, and tradition, and delusion, and appearance, that alluvion which covers the globe, through Paris and London, through New York and Boston and Concord, through Church and State, through poetry and philosophy and religion, till we come to a hard bottom and rocks in place, which we can call *reality*, and say, "This is, and no mistake"; and then begin, having a *point d'appui*, below freshet and frost and fire, a place where you might found a wall or a state, or set a lamp-post safely, or perhaps a gauge, not a Nilometer, but a Realometer, that future ages might know how deep a freshet of shams and appearances had gathered from time to time. If you stand right fronting and face to face to a fact, you will see the sun glimmer on both its surfaces, as if it were a cimiter, and feel its sweet edge dividing you through the heart and marrow, and so you will happily conclude your mortal career. Be it life or death, we crave only reality. If we are really dying, let us hear the rattle in our throats and feel cold in the extremities; if we are alive, let us go about our business. —WAL, 91–92

Of what use this measuring of me if [the tailor] does not measure my character, but only the breadth of my shoulders, as if it were a peg to hang the coat on? —WAL, 22

The mass of men lead lives of quiet desperation. What is called resignation is confirmed desperation. From the desperate city you go into the desperate country, and have to console yourself with the bravery of minks and muskrats. A stereotyped but unconscious despair is concealed even under what are called the games and amusements of mankind. There is no play in them, for this comes after work. But it is a characteristic of wisdom not to do desperate things. —WAL, 6

Let men, true to their natures, cultivate the moral affections, lead manly and independent lives; let them make riches the means and not the end of existence, and we shall hear no more of the commercial spirit. The sea will not stagnate, the earth will be as green as ever, and the air as pure. This curious world which we inhabit is more wonderful than that is convenient; more beautiful than it is useful; it is more to be admired and enjoyed than used. The order of things should be somewhat reversed; the seventh should be man's day of toil, wherein to earn his living by the sweat of his brow; and the other six his Sabbath of the affections and the soul—in which to range this widespread garden, and drink in the soft influences and sublime revelations of Nature.[13]

We can only live healthily the life the gods assign us. I must receive my life as passively as the willow leaf that flutters over the brook. I must not be for myself, but God's work, and that is always good. I will wait the breezes patiently, and grow as Nature shall determine. My fate cannot but be grand so. We may live the life of a plant or an animal, without living an animal life. This constant and universal content of the animal comes of resting quietly in God's palm. I feel as if I could at any time resign my life and the responsibility of living into God's hands, and become as innocent, free from care, as a plant or stone. —JOU i, 326–27

I went to the woods because I wished to live deliberately, to front only the essential facts of life, and see if I could not learn what it had to teach, and not, when I came to die, discover that I had not lived. I did not wish to live what was not life, living is so dear; nor did I wish to practice resignation, unless it was quite necessary. I wanted to live deep and suck out all the marrow of life, to live so sturdily and Spartan-like as to put to rout all that was not life, to cut a broad swath and shave close, to drive life into a corner, and reduce it to its lowest terms, and, if it proved to be mean, why then to get the whole and genuine meanness of it, and publish its meanness to the world; or if it were sublime, to know it by experience, and be able to give a true account of it in my next excursion. —WAL, 85

I left the woods [Walden] for as good a reason as I went there. Perhaps it seemed to me that I had several more lives to live, and could not spare any more time for that one. It is remarkable how easily and insensibly we fall into a particular route, and make a beaten track for ourselves. I had not lived there a week before my feet wore a path from my door to the pond-side; and though it is five or six years since I trod it, it is still quite distinct. It is true, I fear, that others may have fallen into it, and so helped to keep it open. The surface of the earth is soft and impressible by the feet of men; and so with the paths which the mind travels. How worn and dusty, then, must be the highways of the world, how deep the ruts of tradition and conformity! I did not wish to take a cabin passage, but rather to go before the mast and on the deck of the world, for there I could best see the moonlight amid the mountains. I do not wish to go below now.

I learned this, at least, by my experiment: that if one advances confidently in the direction of his dreams, and endeavors to live the life which he has imagined, he will meet with a success unexpected in common hours. He will put some things behind, will pass an invisible boundary; new, universal, and more liberal laws will begin to establish themselves around and within him; or the old laws be expanded, and interpreted in his favor in a more liberal sense, and he will live with the license of a higher order of beings. —WAL, 302–3

When Nature ceases to be supernatural to a man, what will he do then? Of what worth is human life, if its actions are no longer to have this sublime and unexplored scenery? Who will build a cottage and dwell in it with enthusiasm, if not in the Elysian fields? —PJ i, 481

One day, when my axe had come off and I had cut a green hickory for a wedge, driving it with a stone, and had placed the whole to soak in a pond-hole in order to swell the wood, I saw a striped snake run into the water, and he lay on the bottom, apparently without inconvenience, as long as I stayed there, or more than a quarter of an hour; perhaps because he had not yet fairly come out of the torpid state. It appeared to me that for a like reason men remain in their present low and primitive condition; but if they should feel the influence of the spring of springs arousing them, they would of necessity rise to a higher and more ethereal life.

—WAL, 38

SIMPLE LIVING

In proportion as he simplifies his life, the laws of the universe will appear less complex, and solitude will not be solitude, nor poverty poverty, nor weakness weakness. If you have built castles in the air, your work need not be lost; that is where they should be. Now put the foundations under them. — WAL, 303

I do believe in simplicity. It is astonishing as well as sad, how many trivial affairs even the wisest man thinks he must attend to in a day; how singular an affair he thinks he must omit. . . . So simplify the problem of life, distinguish the necessary and the real. Probe the earth to see where your main roots run. . . .

—Letter to Harrison Blake, LSS, 36

In short, I am convinced, both by faith and experience, that to maintain one's self on this earth is not a hardship but a pastime, if we will live simply and wisely; as the pursuits of the simpler nations are still the sports of the more artificial. It is not necessary that a man should earn his living by the sweat of his brow, unless he sweats easier than I do. —WAL, 65–66

I am convinced, that if all men were to live as simply as I then did [at Walden], thieving and robbery would be unknown. These take place only in communities where some have got more than is sufficient while others have not enough. —WAL, 163

If you are a seer, whenever you meet a man you will see all that he owns, ay, and much that he pretends to disown, behind him, even to his kitchen furniture and all the trumpery which he saves and will not burn, and he will appear to be harnessed to it and making what headway he can. . . . It would surpass the powers of a well man nowadays to take up his bed and walk, and I should certainly advise a sick one to lay down his bed and run. —WAL, 61

A man who has at length found something to do will not need to get a new suit to do it in; for him the old will do. . . . —WAL, 20

I tried to help him [John Field, a local farmer] with my experience, telling him that he was one of my nearest neighbors, and that I too, who came a-fishing here, and looked like a loafer, was getting my living like himself; that I lived in a tight, light, and clean house, which hardly cost more than the annual rent of such a ruin as his commonly amounts to; and how, if he chose, he might in a month or two build himself a palace of his own; that I did not use tea, nor coffee, nor butter, nor milk, nor fresh meat, and so did not have to work to get them; again, as I did not work hard, I did not have to eat hard, and it cost me but a trifle for my food; but as he began with tea, and coffee, and butter, and milk, and beef, he had to work hard to pay for them, and when he had worked hard he had to eat hard again to repair the waste of his system—and so it was as broad as it was long, indeed it was broader than it was long, for he was discontented and wasted his life into the bargain; and yet he had rated it as a gain in coming to America, that here you could get tea, and coffee, and meat every day. But the only true America is that country where you are at liberty to pursue such a mode of life as may enable you to do without these, and where the state does not endeavor to compel you to sustain the slavery and war and other superfluous expenses which directly or indirectly result from the use of such things. For I purposely talked to him as if he were a philosopher, or desired to be one. —WAL, 192

Not long since I was present at the auction of a deacon's effects, for his life had not been ineffectual. . . . As usual, a great proportion was trumpery which had begun to accumulate in his father's day. Among the rest was a dried tapeworm. And now, after lying half a century in his garret and other dust holes, these things were not burned; instead of a *bonfire*, or purifying destruction of them, there was an *auction*, or increasing of them.

The neighbors eagerly collected to view them, bought them all, and carefully transported them to their garrets and dust holes, to lie there till their estates are settled, when they will start again.
— WAL, 62–63

Remember thy Creator in the days of thy youth. Rise free from care before the dawn, and seek adventures. Let the noon find thee by other lakes, and the night overtake thee everywhere at home. There are no larger fields than these, no worthier games than may here be played. Grow wild according to thy nature, like these sedges and brakes, which will never become English hay. Let the thunder rumble; what if it threaten ruin to farmers' crops? That is not its errand to thee. Take shelter under the cloud, while they flee to carts and sheds. Let not to get a living be thy trade, but thy sport. Enjoy the land, but own it not. Through want of enterprise and faith men are where they are, buying and selling, and spending their lives like serfs. — WAL, 195

Let him who has work to do recollect that the object of clothing is, first, to retain the vital heat, and secondly, in the state of society, to cover nakedness. . . . No man ever stood the lower in my estimation for having a patch in his clothes. — WAL, 19

Every generation laughs at the old fashions, but follows religiously the new. —WAL, 23

THE HEAVENLY AND THE TERRESTRIAL

One of Thoreau's recurring themes in his letters to Harrison Blake (see the introduction) was the need to balance the legitimate claims of the world—"getting a living"—with those of the spirit. A natural contemplative drawn powerfully to solitude, Thoreau nonetheless was deeply committed to social action. At times, he had to guard himself from allowing his political passions to overrun his interior life, as happened when he publicly defended John Brown during Brown's 1859 trial for sedition.

Happy the man who observes the heavenly and the terrestrial law in just proportion; whose every faculty, from the soles of his feet to the crown of his head, obeys the laws of its level; who neither stoops nor goes on tiptoe, but lives a balanced life, acceptable to nature and to God. — Letter to Harrison Blake, LSS, 47

There is little or nothing to be remembered written on the subject of getting an honest living. Neither the New Testament nor Poor Richard speaks to our condition. I cannot think of a single page which entertains, much less answers, the questions which I put to myself on this subject. How to make the getting our living poetic! for if it is not poetic, it is not life but death that we get. Is it that men are too disgusted with their experience to speak of it? . . . The most practically important of all questions, it seems to me, is how shall I get my living, and yet I find little or nothing said to the purpose in any book. . . . One would think, from looking at literature, that this question had never disturbed a solitary individual's musings. . . .

If it were not that I desire to do something here—accomplish some work—I should certainly prefer to suffer and die rather than be at the pains to get a living by the modes men propose.

—JOU ii,164

For more than five years I maintained myself thus solely by the labor of my hands, and I found that, by working about six weeks in a year, I could meet all the expenses of living. The whole of my winters, as well as most of my summers, I had free and clear for study. I have thoroughly tried school-keeping, and found that my expenses were in proportion, or rather out of proportion, to my income, for I was obliged to dress and train, not to say think and believe, accordingly, and I lost my time into the bargain. As I did not teach for the good of my fellow-men, but simply for a livelihood, this was a failure. I have tried trade; but I found that it would take ten years to get underway in that, and that then I should probably be on my way to the devil. I was actually afraid that I might by that time be doing what is called a good business. When formerly I was looking about to see what I could do for a living, some sad experience in conforming to the wishes of friends being fresh in my mind to tax my ingenuity, I thought often and seriously of picking huckleberries; that surely I could do, and its small profits might suffice—for my greatest skill has been to want but little—so little capital it required, so little distraction from my wonted moods, I foolishly thought. While my acquaintances went unhesitatingly into trade or the professions, I contemplated this occupation as most like theirs; ranging the hills all summer to pick the berries which came in my way, and thereafter carelessly dispose of them; so, to keep the flocks of Admetus. I also dreamed that I might gather the wild herbs, or carry evergreens to such villagers as loved to be reminded of the woods, even to the city, by hay-cart loads. But I have since learned that trade curses everything it handles; and though you trade in messages from heaven, the whole curse of trade attaches to the business.

—WAL, 64–65

As for conforming outwardly, and living your own life inwardly, I do not think much of that. . . . It is a greater strain than any soul can long endure. When you get God to pulling one way and the devil the other, . . . almost any timber will give.

— Letter to Harrison Blake, LSS, 62

How prompt we are to satisfy the hunger and thirst of our bodies; how slow to satisfy the hunger and thirst of our *souls*. . . . He alone is the truly enterprising and practical man who succeeds in *maintaining* his soul here. Haven't we our everlasting life to get? And isn't that the only excuse at last for eating, drinking, sleeping, or even carrying an umbrella when it rains?

—Letter to Harrison Blake, LSS, 85–86

I would fain say something, not so much concerning the Chinese and Sandwich Islanders as you who read these pages, who are said to live in New England; something about your condition, especially your outward condition or circumstances in this world, in this town, what it is, whether it is necessary that it be as bad as it is, whether it cannot be improved as well as not. I have traveled a good deal in Concord; and everywhere, in shops, and offices, and fields, the inhabitants have appeared to me to be doing penance in a thousand remarkable ways. . . .

I see young men, my townsmen, whose misfortune it is to have inherited farms, houses, barns, cattle, and farming tools; for these are more easily acquired than got rid of. Better if they had been born in the open pasture and suckled by a wolf, that they might have seen with clearer eyes what field they were called to labor in. Who made them serfs of the soil? Why should they eat their sixty acres, when man is condemned to eat only his peck of dirt? Why should they begin digging their graves as soon as they are born? . . . —WAL, 2–3

After spending four or five days surveying, . . . I especially feel the necessity of putting myself in communication with nature again, to recover my tone, to withdraw out of the wearying and unprofitable world of affairs. . . . Having waded in the very shallowest stream of time, I would now bathe my temples in eternity. I wish again to participate in the serenity of nature, to share the happiness of the river and the woods. I thus from time to time break off my connection with eternal truths and go with a shallow stream of human affairs, grinding at the mill of the Philistines; but when my task is done, with never failing confidence, I devote myself to the infinite again. —JOU ix, 205

But men labor under a mistake. The better part of the man is soon plowed into the soil for compost. By a seeming fate, commonly called necessity, they are employed, as it says in an old book, laying up treasures which moth and rust will corrupt and thieves break through and steal. It is a fool's life, as they will find when they get to the end of it, if not before. WAL, 2–3

What is that other kind of life to which I am thus continually allured? which alone I love? Is it a life for this world? Can a man feed and clothe himself gloriously who keeps only the truth steadily before him? Who calls in no evil to his aid? Are there duties which necessarily interfere with the serene perception of truth? —JOU ii, 268

I have been surveying for twenty or thirty days, living coarsely, even as respects my diet, for I find that that will always alter to suit my employment—indeed, leading a quite trivial life; and tonight, for the first time, had made a fire in my chamber and endeavored to return to myself. I wished to ally myself to the powers that rule the universe. I wished to dive into some deep stream of thoughtful and devoted life, which meandered through retired and fertile meadows far from towns. I wished to do again, or for once, things quite congenial to my highest, inmost, and most sacred nature, . . . to let my life flow in its proper channels, with its proper currents. —JOU iii, 133

Most men, even in this comparatively free country, through mere ignorance and mistake, are so occupied with the factitious cares and superfluously coarse labors of life that its finer fruits cannot be plucked by them. Their fingers, from excessive toil, are too clumsy and tremble too much for that. Actually, the laboring man has not leisure for a true integrity day by day; he cannot afford to sustain the manliest relations to men; his labor would be depreciated in the market. He has no time to be anything but a machine. —WAL, 4

SOLITUDE AND SILENCE

I am invited to take some party of ladies or gentlemen on an excursion—to walk or sail or the like—but by all kinds of evasions I omit it, and am thought to be rude and unaccommodating therefore. They do not consider that the wood-path and the boat are my studio, where I maintain a sacred solitude and cannot admit promiscuous company. . . . Ask me for a certain number of dollars if you will, but do not ask me for my afternoons.

—JOU xii, 332–33

I have a great deal of company in my house; especially in the morning, when nobody calls. . . . I am no more lonely than the loon in the pond that laughs so loud, or than Walden Pond itself. . . . God is alone—but the devil, he is far from being alone;

he sees a great deal of company; he is legion. I am no more lonely than a single mullein or dandelion in a pasture, or a bean leaf, or sorrel, or a horsefly, or a bumblebee. I am no more lonely than the Mill Brook, or a weathercock, or the north star, or the south wind, or an April shower, or a January thaw, or the first spider in a new house. —WAL, 129–30

I go through the woods toward the Cliffs along the side of the Well Meadow Field.

There is nothing so sanative, so poetic, as a walk in the woods and fields even now, when I meet none abroad for pleasure. Nothing so inspires me and excites such serene and profitable thought. . . . I come to myself, I once more feel myself grandly related, and that cold and solitude are friends of mine. I suppose that this value, in my case, is equivalent to what others get by churchgoing and prayer. I come to my solitary woodland walk as the homesick go home. I thus dispose of the superfluous and see things as they are, grand and beautiful. I have told many that I walk every day about half the daylight, but I think they do not believe it. . . . I come out to these solitudes, where the problem of existence is simplified. I get away a mile or two from the town into the stillness and solitude of nature, with rocks, trees, weeds, snow about me. I enter some glade in the woods, perchance, where a few weeds and dry leaves alone lift themselves above the surface of the snow, and it is as if I had come to an open window. I see out and around myself. . . . This is what I go out to seek. It is as if I always met in those places some grand, serene, immortal, infinitely encouraging, though invisible, companion, and walked with him. There at last my nerves are steadied, my senses and my mind do their office.

—JOU ix, 208–9

I find it wholesome to be alone the greater part of the time. To be in company, even with the best, is soon wearisome and dissipating. I love to be alone. I never found the companion that was so companionable as solitude. We are for the most part more lonely when we go abroad among men than when we stay in our chambers. A man thinking or working is always alone, let him be where he will. Solitude is not measured by the miles of space that intervene between a man and his fellows. —WAL, 128

It is not that we love to be alone, but that we love to soar, and when we do soar, the company grows thinner and thinner till there is none at all. It is either the Tribune on the plain, a sermon on the mount, or a very private *ecstasy* still higher up. We are not the less to aim at the summits, though the multitude does not ascend them. —Letter to Harrison Blake, LSS, 136

I think that I love society as much as most, and am ready enough to fasten myself like a bloodsucker for the time to any full-blooded man that comes in my way. I am naturally no hermit, but might possibly sit out the sturdiest frequenter of the bar-room, if my business called me thither. —WAL, 132

You think that I am impoverishing myself by withdrawing from men, but in my solitude I have woven for myself a silken web or *chrysalis*, and, nymph-like, shall ere long burst forth a more perfect creature, fitted for a higher society. —JOU ix, 246

Sometimes, after staying in a village parlor till the family had all retired, I have returned to the woods, and, partly with a view to the next day's dinner, spent the hours of midnight fishing from a boat by moonlight, serenaded by owls and foxes, and hearing, from time to time, the creaking note of some unknown bird close at hand. These experiences were very memorable and valuable to me—anchored in forty feet of water, and twenty or thirty rods from the shore, surrounded sometimes by thousands of small perch and shiners, dimpling the surface with their tails in the moonlight, and communicating by a long flaxen line with mysterious nocturnal fishes which had their dwelling forty feet below, or sometimes dragging sixty feet of line about the pond as I drifted in the gentle night breeze, now and then feeling a slight vibration along it, indicative of some life prowling about its extremity, of dull uncertain blundering purpose there, and slow to make up its mind. At length you slowly raise, pulling hand over hand, some horned pout squeaking and squirming to the upper air. It was very queer, especially in dark nights, when your thoughts had wandered to vast and cosmogonal themes in other spheres, to feel this faint jerk, which came to interrupt your dreams and link you to Nature again. It seemed as if I might next cast my line upward into the air, as well as downward into this element, which was scarcely more dense. Thus I caught two fishes as it were with one hook. —WAL, 165–66

For what reason have I this vast range and circuit, some square miles of unfrequented forest, for my privacy, abandoned to me by men? My nearest neighbor is a mile distant, and no house is visible from any place but the hill-tops within half a mile of my own. I have my horizon bounded by woods all to myself; a distant view of the railroad where it touches the pond on the one hand, and of the fence which skirts the woodland road on the other. But for the most part it is as solitary where I live as on the prairies. It is as much Asia or Africa as New England. I have, as it were, my own sun and moon and stars, and a little world all to myself. —WAL, 123

As the truest society approaches always nearer to solitude, so the most excellent speech finally falls into Silence. Silence is audible to all men, at all times, and in all places. . . . Creation has not displaced her, but is her visible framework and foil. All sounds are her servants, and purveyors, proclaiming not only that their mistress is, but is a rare mistress, and earnestly to be sought after. . . . She is Truth's speaking-trumpet, the sole oracle, the true Delphi and Dodona, which kings and courtiers would do well to consult, nor will they be balked by an ambiguous answer. For through her all revelations have been made, and just in proportion as men have consulted her oracle within, they have obtained a clear insight, and their age has been marked as an enlightened one. . . . It were vain for me to endeavor to interrupt the Silence. She cannot be done into English. For six thousand years men have translated her with what fidelity belonged to each, and still she is little better than a sealed book. —WCM, 391–93

Silence is the communing of a conscious soul with itself. If the soul attend for a moment to its own infinity, then and there is silence. . . .

Silence is ever less strange than noise, lurking amid the boughs of the hemlock or pine just in proportion as we find ourselves there. The nuthatch, tapping the upright trunks by our side, is only a partial spokesman for the solemn stillness.

She is always at hand with her wisdom, by roadsides and street corners; lurking in belfries, the cannon's mouth, and the wake of the earthquake; gathering up and fondling their puny din in her ample bosom.

Those divine sounds which are uttered to our inward ear—which are breathed in with the zephyr or reflected from the lake—come to us noiselessly, bathing the temples of the soul, as we stand motionless amid the rocks. —JOU i, 64–65

FRIENDSHIP

A Friend is one who incessantly pays us the compliment of expecting from us all the virtues, and who can appreciate them in us. It takes two to speak the truth—one to speak, and another to hear. . . .

But sometimes we are said to *love* another, that is, to stand in a true relation to him, so that we give the best to, and receive the best from, him. Between whom there is hearty truth, there is love; and in proportion to our truthfulness and confidence in one another, our lives are divine and miraculous, and answer to our ideal. There are passages of affection in our intercourse with mortal men and women, such as no prophecy had taught us to expect, which transcend our earthly life, and anticipate Heaven for us. What is this Love that may come right into the middle of a prosaic Goffstown day, equal to any of the gods? that discovers a new world, fair and fresh and eternal, occupying the place of the old one. . . ?

Impatient and uncertain lovers think that they must say or do something kind whenever they meet; they must never be cold.

But they who are Friends do not do what they *think* they must, but what they *must*. Even their Friendship is to some extent but a sublime phenomenon to them. . . .

There are times when we have had enough even of our Friends, when we begin inevitably to profane one another, and must withdraw religiously into solitude and silence, the better to prepare ourselves for a loftier intimacy. Silence is the ambrosial night in the intercourse of Friends, in which their sincerity is recruited and takes deeper root. . . .

The only danger in Friendship is that it will end. It is a delicate plant, though a native. The least unworthiness, even if it be unknown to one's self, vitiates it. Let the Friend know that those faults which he observes in his Friend his own faults attract. There is no rule more invariable than that we are paid for our suspicions by finding what we suspected. By our narrowness and prejudices we say, I will have so much and such of you, my Friend, no more. Perhaps there are none charitable, none disinterested, none wise, noble, and heroic enough, for a true and lasting Friendship.

—WCM, 267–77

Friendship is not so kind as is imagined. It has not much human blood in it. It has a certain disregard for men . . . while it purifies the atmosphere like electricity. . . . It was established before religion, for men are not friends in religion, but over and through it, and it records no apostasy or repentance, but there is a certain divine and innocent and perennial health about it. A certain disregard for the Christian duties and humanities is consistent with its perfect integrity. . . . It's charity generosity—it's virtue nobleness—it's religion trust. . . . It is not for the friend to be just. . . . But to be only a large and free existence representative of humanity. —PJ i, 88

As surely as the sunset in my latest November shall translate me to the ethereal world, and remind me of the ruddy morning of youth; as surely as the last strain of music which falls on my decaying ear shall make age to be forgotten, or, in short, the manifold influences of nature survive during the term of our natural life, so surely my Friend shall forever be my Friend, and reflect a ray of God to me, and time shall foster and adorn and consecrate our Friendship, no less than the ruins of temples. As I love nature, as I love singing birds, and gleaming stubble, and flowing rivers, and morning and evening, and summer and winter, I love thee, my Friend.

—WCM, 285

3

The Spiritual Life

Though irreligious by temperament, Thoreau was a lifelong spiritual seeker who sought contact with the divine in the natural world rather than through liturgical worship or scriptural revelation. His self-proclaimed "profession" was to always be on the alert "to find God in nature," so that his daily, meditative walks through the Concord woodlands often served as sacramental explorations of a sacred creation. Thoreau's spiritual life also included daily journal writing, recording "the ebbs and flows" of his soul, as well as transcendent periods of spiritual transport in which he felt himself in ecstatic communication "with the gods."

CONTEMPLATION

He is the rich man and enjoys the fruits of riches, who, summer and winter forever, can find delight in the contemplation of his soul. I could look as unweariedly up to that cope (sky) as into the heavens of a summer day or a winter night. When I hear this bell ring, I am carried back to years and sabbaths when I was newer and more innocent, I fear, than now, and it seems to me as if there were a world within a world. . . . The whole duty of life is contained in the question how to respire and aspire both at once.

—JOU i, 300

Heaven is the inmost place. The good have not to travel far. . . . I wish I could be as still as God is. I can recall to my mind the stillest summer hour, in which the grasshopper sings over the mulleins, and there is a valor in that time the memory of which is armor that can laugh at any blow of fortune. . . . —JOU i, 301

If we can listen we shall hear. By reverently listening to the inner voice, we may reinstate ourselves on the pinnacle of humanity.
—JOU i, 177

Sometimes, in a summer morning, having taken my accustomed bath, I sat in my sunny doorway from sunrise till noon, rapt in a reverie, amidst the pines and hickories and sumachs, in undisturbed solitude and stillness, while the birds sang around or flitted noiseless through the house, until by the sun falling in at my west window, or the noise of some traveler's wagon on the distant highway, I was reminded of the lapse of time. I grew in those seasons like corn in the night, and they were far better than any work of the hands would have been. They were not time subtracted from my life, but so much over and above my usual allowance. I realized what the Orientals mean by contemplation and the forsaking of works. —WAL, 105–6

Our limbs indeed have room enough, but it is our souls that rust in a corner. Let us migrate interiorly without intermission, and pitch our tent each day nearer the western horizon. The really fertile soils and luxuriant prairies lie on this side of the Alleghenies.
—JOU i, 131

If you would learn to speak all tongues and conform to the customs of all nations . . . obey the precept of the old philosopher, and Explore thyself. —WAL, 30

It behooves us to be attentive. If by watching all day and all night I may detect some trace of the ineffable, then will it not be worth the while to watch? Watch and pray without ceasing, but not necessarily in sadness. We are surrounded by a rich and fertile mystery. May we not probe it, pry into it, employ ourselves about it, a little?. . . Go in search of the springs of life, and you will get exercise enough. —JOU ii, 471–72

When I look back eastward over the world, it seems to be all in repose. Arabia, Persia, Hindostan are the land of contemplation. Those Eastern nations have perfected the luxury of idleness. . . .

In my brain is the Sanskrit which contains the history of the primitive times. The Vedas and their Angas are not so ancient as my serenest contemplations. My mind contemplates them, as Brahma his scribe. —JOU i, 343–44

Be rather the Mungo Park [British explorer], the Lewis and Clark and Frobisher, of your own streams and oceans; explore your own higher latitudes. . . . Nay, be a Columbus to whole new continents and worlds within you, opening new channels, not of trade, but of thought. . . . There are continents and seas in the moral world to which every man is an isthmus or an inlet, yet unexplored by him, but that it is easier to sail many thousand miles through cold and storm and cannibals, in a government ship, with five hundred men and boys to assist one, than it is to explore the private sea, the Atlantic and Pacific Ocean of one's being alone. —WAL, 300–301

SPIRITUAL PRACTICES

Although conditioned by a Calvinist theology unsympathetic to monastic traditions, Thoreau arranged his daily life around a quasi-monastic set of spiritual disciplines common both to traditional Catholic contemplatives and Indian sadhus (renunciates). He embraced a life of material simplicity, sexual restraint, and "obedience to the all-just laws" of the Creator, unintentionally mirroring the classical triad of monastic vows—poverty, chastity, and obedience—articulated in the sixth-century Rule of St. Benedict and followed today by most Catholic orders. Thoreau's practices were also inspired by his encounter with Indian scriptures like the Bhagavad Gita, *especially their emphasis on self-denial, contemplation, and nonattachment. Thoreau might be understood in this sense as a kind of unrobed or contemplative monk whose cloister was the woods and waterways of the Concord countryside.*

They are not ordinary practices which can bring light into the soul. —JOU ii, 190–91

The whole duty of man may be expressed in one line—Make to yourself a perfect body. —PJ iii, 138

I find that I conciliate the gods by some sacrament as bathing or abstemiousness in diet, or rising early—and directly they smile on me. These are my sacraments. —PJ iii, 4

I never feel that I am inspired unless my body is also. It too spurns a tame and commonplace life. They are fatally mistaken who think while they strive with their minds, that they may suffer their bodies to stagnate in luxury or sloth. The body is the first proselyte the Soul makes. Our life is but the Soul made known by its fruits—the body. —PJ i, 137

The Muni [seeker] who desires his final emancipation will have care evening and morning to subdue his senses, to fix his mind on the divine essence, and to transport himself by the force of his soul to the eternal abode of Vishnu [God]. Although he may have engaged in works, he does not wear the clog of them, because his soul is not attached to them. . . . Free in this world, as the birds in the air, disengaged from every kind of chain. —JOU ii, 191

No method nor discipline can supersede the necessity of being forever on the alert. What is a course of history or philosophy, or poetry, no matter how well selected, or the best society, or the most admirable routine of life, compared with the discipline of looking always at what is to be seen? Will you be a reader, a student merely, or a seer? Read your fate, see what is before you, and walk on into futurity. —WAL, 105

All sensuality is one, though it takes many forms; all purity is one. It is the same whether a man eat, or drink, or cohabit, or sleep sensually. They are but one appetite, and we only need to see a person do any one of these things to know how great a sensualist he is. The impure can neither stand nor sit with purity. . . . Nature is hard to be overcome, but she must be overcome. What avails it that you are Christian, if you are not purer than the heathen, if you deny yourself no more, if you are not more religious? —WAL, 207

In earlier ages, in some countries, every function was reverently spoken of and regulated by law. Nothing was too trivial for the Hindu lawgiver [Manu], however offensive it may be to modern taste. He teaches how to eat, drink, cohabit, void excrement and urine, and the like, elevating what is mean, and does not falsely excuse himself by calling these things trifles.

Every man is the builder of a temple, called his body, to the god he worships, after a style purely his own, nor can he get off by hammering marble instead. We are all sculptors and painters, and our material is our own flesh and blood and bones. Any nobleness begins at once to refine a man's features, any meanness or sensuality to imbrute them. —WAL, 207–8

Whatever my own practice may be, I have no doubt that it is a part of the destiny of the human race, in its gradual improvement, to leave off eating animals, as surely as the savage tribes have left off eating each other when they came in contact with the more civilized. —WAL, 201–3

No method or discipline can supersede the necessity of being forever on the alert. What is a course of history when one is reminded that he may be a *Seer,* but to keep his eye constantly on the true and real is a discipline that will absorb every other. —JOU i, 279

POVERTY

Cultivate poverty like a garden herb, like sage. Do not trouble yourself much to get new things, whether clothes or friends. Turn the old; return to them. Things do not change; we change. Sell your clothes and keep your thoughts. God will see that you do not want society. . . . Do not seek so anxiously to be developed, to subject yourself to many influences to be played on; it is all dissipation. Humility like darkness reveals the heavenly lights. The shadows of poverty and meanness gather around us, "and lo! Creation widens to our view." . . . Moreover, if you are restricted in your range by poverty, if you cannot buy books and newspapers, for instance, you are but confined to the most significant and vital experiences; you are compelled to deal with the material which yields the most sugar and the most starch. It is life near the bone which is sweetest. . . . Money is not required to buy one necessary of the soul. . . .

Rather than love, than money, than fame, give me truth.

—WAL, 307–9

Again and again I congratulate myself on my so called poverty. I was almost disappointed yesterday to find thirty dollars in my desk which I did not know that I possessed, though now I should be sorry to lose it. . . .

By poverty, *i.e.*, simplicity of life and fewness of incidents, I am solidified and crystallized, as a vapor or liquid by cold. It is a singular concentration of strength and energy and flavor. . . . My diffuse and vaporous life becomes as the frost leaves . . . radiant as gems on the weeds and stubble in a winter morning. You think that I am impoverishing myself by withdrawing from men, but in my solitude I have woven for myself a silken web or *chrysalis*, and, nymph-like, shall ere long burst forth a more perfect creature, fitted for a higher society. By simplicity, commonly called poverty, my life is concentrated and so becomes organized. . . .

Each man and woman is a veritable god or goddess, but to the mass of their fellows disguised. There is only one in each case who sees through the disguise. That one who does not stand so near to any man as to see the divinity in him is truly alone.

—JOU ix, 246–50

Most of the luxuries, and many of the so-called comforts of life, are not only not indispensable, but positive hindrances to the elevation of mankind. With respect to luxuries and comforts, the wisest have ever lived a more simple and meager life than the poor. The ancient philosophers, Chinese, Hindu, Persian, and Greek, were a class than which none has been poorer in outward riches, none so rich in inward. . . .To be a philosopher is not merely to have subtle thoughts, nor even to found a school, but so to love wisdom as to live according to its dictates, a life of simplicity, independence, magnanimity, and trust. It is to solve some of the problems of life, not only theoretically, but practically.

—WAL, 12–13

What you call bareness and poverty is to me simplicity. God could not be unkind to me if he should try. . . . I love best to have each thing in its season only, and enjoy doing without it at all other times. It is the greatest of all advantages to enjoy no advantage at all. I find it invariably true, the poorer I am, the richer I am. What you consider my disadvantage, I consider my advantage. While you are pleased to get knowledge and culture in many ways, I am delighted to think that I am getting rid of them. I have never got over my surprise that I should have been born into the most estimable place in all the world, and in the very nick of time, too.

—JOU ix, 160

CONTINENCE

Thoreau remained a bachelor all his life and embraced his chastity as a spiritual discipline, arguing that it sublimated "the generative energy," which, when transmuted, he wrote, "invigorates and inspires."[14]

Chastity is perpetual acquaintance with the All. —JOU ix, 246

Who knows what sort of life would result if we had attained to purity? If I knew so wise a man as could teach me purity I would go to seek him forthwith. "A command over our passions, and over the external senses of the body, and good acts, are declared by the Ved [Indian scriptures] to be indispensable in the mind's approximation to God." Yet the spirit can for the time pervade and control every member and function of the body, and transmute what in form is the grossest sensuality into purity and devotion. The generative energy, which, when we are loose, dissipates and makes us unclean, when we are continent invigorates and inspires us. Chastity is the flowering of man; and what are called Genius, Heroism, Holiness, and the like, are but various fruits which succeed it. Man flows at once to God when the channel of purity is open. By turns our purity inspires and our impurity casts us down. He is blessed who is assured that the animal is dying out in him day by day, and the divine being established.

— WAL, 206

In September 1852, Harrison Blake, Thoreau's spiritual correspondent since 1848, was married. As a wedding "gift," Thoreau sent Blake notes on the subject of sex and chastity that he had written in his journal during the spring of 1845. The letter is remarkably frank for its time in treatment of sex and striking in its endorsement of voluntary chastity, a feature of medieval monasticism long discredited by the Protestant Reformation.

The subject of sex is a remarkable one, since, though its phenomena concern us so much, both directly and indirectly, and, sooner or later, it occupies the thoughts of all, yet all mankind, as it were, agree to be silent about it, at least the sexes commonly one to another. One of the most interesting of all human facts is veiled more completely than any mystery. . . .

In a pure society, the subject of copulation would not be so often avoided from shame and not from reverence, winked out of sight, and hinted at only, but treated naturally and simply—perhaps simply avoided, like the kindred mysteries. If it cannot be spoken of for shame, how can it be acted of? But, doubtless, there is far more purity, as well as more impurity, than is apparent.

Men commonly couple with their idea of marriage a slight degree at least of sensuality; but every lover, the world over, believes in its inconceivable purity.

If it is the result of a pure love, there can be nothing sensual in marriage. Chastity is something positive, not negative. It is the virtue of the married especially. All lusts or base pleasures must give place to loftier delights. They who meet as superior beings cannot perform the deeds of inferior ones. The deeds of love are less questionable than any action of an individual can be, for, it being founded on the rarest mutual respect, the parties incessantly stimulate each other to loftier and purer life, and the act in which they are associated must be pure and noble indeed, for innocence and purity can have no equal. In this relation we deal with one whom we respect more religiously even than we respect our better selves, and we shall necessarily conduct as in the presence of God. What presence can be more awful to the lover than that of his beloved? . . .

Can love be in aught allied to dissipation? Let us love by refusing, not accepting one another. Love and lust are far asunder. The one is good, the other bad. When the affectionate sympathize by their higher natures, there is love; but there is danger that they will sympathize by their lower natures, and then there is lust. It is not necessary that this be deliberate, hardly even conscious; but, in the close contact of affection, there is danger that we may stain and pollute one another, for we cannot embrace but with an entire embrace. . . .

The *luxury* of affection—there's the danger. There must be some nerve and heroism in our love, as of a winter morning. In the religion of all nations a purity is hinted at, which, I fear, men never attain to. We may love and not elevate one another. The love that takes us as it finds us degrades us. What watch we must keep over the fairest and purest of our affections, lest there be some taint about them. May we so love as never to have occasion to repent of our love. . . .

Flowers, which, by their infinite use and fragrance, celebrate the marriage of the plants, are intended for the symbol of the open and unsuspected beauty of all true marriage, when man's flowering season arrives.

Virginity, too, is a budding flower, and by an impure marriage the virgin is deflowered. Whoever loves flowers, loves virgins and chastity. Love and lust are as far asunder as a flower garden is from a brothel. . . .

The intercourse of the sexes, I have dreamed, is incredibly beautiful, too fair to be remembered. I have had thoughts about it, but they are among the most fleeting and irrecoverable in my experience. It is strange that men will talk of miracles, revelation, inspiration, and the like, as things past, while love remains.

A true marriage will differ in no wise from illumination. In all perception of the truth there is a divine ecstasy, an inexpressible delirium of joy, as when a youth embraces his betrothed virgin. The ultimate delights of a true marriage are one with this.

No wonder that, out of such a union, not as end, but as accompaniment, comes the undying race of man. The womb is a most fertile soil.

Some have asked if the stock of men could not be improved—if they could not be bred as cattle. Let Love be purified, and all the rest will follow. A pure love is thus, indeed, the panacea for all the ills of the world.

The only excuse for reproduction is improvement. Nature abhors repetition. Beasts merely propagate their kind; but the offspring of noble men and women will be superior to themselves, as their aspirations are. By their fruits ye shall know them.

—Letter to Harrison Blake, LSS, 76–80

OBEDIENCE TO CONSCIENCE

There is but one obligation and that is the obligation to obey the highest dictate. None can lay me under another which will supersede this. The gods have given me these years without any encumbrance—society has no mortgage on them. If any man assist me in the way of the world, let him derive satisfaction from the deed itself. For I think I never shall have dissolved my prior obligations to God. —JOU i, 279

Indeed, it is by obeying the suggestions of a higher light within you that you escape from yourself and, in the transit, as it were, see with the unworn sides of your eye, travel totally new paths. . . .

—JOU ix, 37–44

There is something proudly thrilling in the thought that this obedience to conscience and trust in God, which is so solemnly preached in extremities and arduous circumstances, is only to retreat to one's self, and rely on our own strength. In trivial circumstances I find myself sufficient to myself, and in the most momentous I have no ally but myself, and must silently put by their harm by my own strength, as I did the former. As my own hand bent aside the willow in my path, so must my single arm put to flight the devil and his angels. God is not our ally when we shrink. . . . If by trusting in God you lose any particle of your vigor, trust in Him no longer. When you trust, do not lay aside your armor, but put it on and buckle it tighter. . . . And there is more of God and divine help in a man's little finger than in idle prayer and trust. —JOU i, 180–81

One cannot too soon forget his errors and misdemeanors; for [to] dwell long upon them is to add to the offense, and repentance and sorrow can only be displaced by somewhat better, and which is as free and original as if they had not been. Not to grieve long for any action, but to go immediately and do freshly and otherwise, subtracts so much from the wrong. Else we may make the delay of repentance the punishment of the sin. But a great nature will not consider its sins as its own, but be more absorbed in the prospect of that valor and virtue for the future which is more properly it, than in those improper actions which, by being sins, discover themselves to be not it. —JOU i, 318

TRANSCENDENCE

If with closed ears and eyes I consult consciousness for a moment, immediately are all walls and barriers dissipated, earth rolls from under me, and I float, by the impetus derived from the earth and the system, a subjective, heavily laden thought, in the midst of an unknown and infinite sea, or else heave and swell like a vast ocean of thought, without rock or headland, where are all riddles solved, all straight lines making there their two ends to meet, eternity and space gambolling familiarly through my depths. I am from the beginning, knowing no end, no aim. No sun illumines me, for I dissolve all lesser lights in my own intenser and steadier light. I am a restful kernel in the magazine of the universe.

Men are constantly dinging in my ears their fair theories and plausible solutions of the universe, but ever there is no help, and I return again to my shoreless, islandless ocean, and fathom unceasingly for a bottom that will hold an anchor, that it may not drag. —JOU i, 53–54

There was a time when the beauty and the music were all within, and I sat and listened to my thoughts, and there was a song in them. I sat for hours on rocks and wrestled with the melody which possessed me. I sat and listened by the hour to a positive though faint and distant music, not sung by any bird, nor vibrating earthly harp. When you walked with a joy which knew not its origin. When you were an organ of which the world was but one poor broken pipe. I lay long on the rocks, foundered like a harp on the seashore, that knows not how it is dealt with. You sat on the earth as on a raft, listening to music that was not of the earth, but which ruled and arranged it. Man *should* be the harp articulate. —JOU vi, 294

Drifting in a sultry day on the sluggish waters of the pond, I almost cease to live and begin to be. A boatman stretched on the deck of his craft and dallying with the noon would be as apt an emblem of eternity for me, as the serpent with his tail in his mouth. I am never so prone to lose my identity. I am dissolved in the haze. —JOU i, 75

We must look on the world with a drowsy and half-shut eye, that it may not be too much in our eye, and rather stand aloof from, than within it. When we are awake to the real world, we are asleep to the actual. The sinful drowse to eternity, the virtuous to time. Manu [an Indian seer] says that the "supreme omnipresent intelligence" is "a spirit which can only be conceived by a mind *slumbering*." Wisdom and holiness always slumber; they are never active in the ways of the world. As in our night dreams we are nearest to awakening, so in our daydreams we are nearest to a supernatural awakening. . . . —JOU i, 229–30

To be calm, to be serene. There is the calmness of the lake when there is not a breath of wind. . . . So it is with us. Sometimes we are clarified and called healthily as we never were before in our lives, not by an opiate, but by some unconscious obedience to the all-just laws, so that we become like a still lake of purest crystal and without an effort our depths are revealed to ourselves. All the world goes by us and is reflected in our deeps. Such clarity! Obtained by such pure means! By simple living, by honesty of purpose. We live and rejoice. I awoke into a music which no one about me heard. Whom shall I thank for it? The luxury of wisdom! The luxury of virtue! Are there any intemperate in these things? I feel my Maker blessing me. —JOU ii, 268–69

As I was entering the Deep Cut [along the Boston–Concord Railroad], the wind, which was conveying a message to me from heaven, dropped it on the wire of the telegraph which it vibrated as it passed. I instantly sat down on a stone at the foot of the telegraph pole and attended to the communication. It merely said: "Bear in mind, Child, and never for an instant forget, that there are higher planes, infinitely higher planes, of life than this thou art now travelling on. Know that the goal is distant, and is upward, and is worthy all your life's efforts to attain to." And then it ceased, and though I sat some minutes longer I heard nothing more. —JOU ii, 497

There are a few sounds still which never fail to affect me. The notes of the wood thrush and the sound of a vibrating chord, these affect me as many sounds once did often, and as almost all should. The strains of the aolian harp and of the wood thrush are the truest and loftiest preachers that I know now left on this earth. I know of no missionaries to us heathen comparable to them. They, as it were, lift us up in spite of ourselves. They intoxicate, they charm us. . . . He that hath ears, let him hear. The contact of sound with a human ear whose hearing is pure and unimpaired is coincident with an ecstasy. Sugar is not so sweet to the palate, as sound to the healthy ear; the hearing of it makes men brave. . . .

These things alone remind me of my immortality, which is else a fable. I hear it, and I realize and see clearly what at other tunes I only dimly remember. I get the value of the earth's extent and the sky's depth. It, as it were, takes me out of my body and gives me the freedom of all bodies and all nature. I leave my body in a trance and accompany the zephyr and the fragrance.

—JOU vi, 39–40

Our ecstatic states, which appear to yield so little fruit, have this value at least: though in the seasons when our genius reigns we may be powerless for expression, yet, in calmer seasons, when our talent is active, the memory of those rarer moods comes to color our picture and is the permanent paint pot, as it were, into which we dip our brush. . . . Our moments of inspiration are not lost though we have no particular poem to show for them; for those experiences have left an indelible impression, and we are ever and anon reminded of them. —JOU ii, 468–69

My desire for knowledge is intermittent, but my desire to bathe my head in atmospheres unknown to my feet is perennial and constant. The highest that we can attain to is not Knowledge, but Sympathy with Intelligence. I do not know that this higher knowledge amounts to anything more definite than a novel and grand surprise on a sudden revelation of the insufficiency of all that we called Knowledge before—a discovery that there are more things in heaven and earth than are dreamed of in our philosophy. It is the lighting up of the mist by the sun. Man cannot *know* in any higher sense than this, any more than he can look serenely and with impunity in the face of the sun. —ESS, 172

This is a delicious evening, when the whole body is one sense, and imbibes delight through every pore. I go and come with a strange liberty in Nature, a part of herself. —WAL, 122

I was always conscious of sounds in nature which my ears could never hear—that I caught but the prelude to a strain. She always retreats as I advance. . . . I never saw to the end, nor heard to the end; but the best part was unseen and unheard.

I am like a feather floating in the atmosphere; on every side is depth unfathomable. —JOU i, 321

Hermit alone: Let me see; where was I? Methinks I was nearly in this frame of mind; the world lay about at this angle. Shall I go to heaven or a-fishing? If I should soon bring this meditation to an end, would another so sweet occasion be likely to offer? I was as near being resolved into the essence of things as ever I was in my life. I fear my thoughts will not come back to me. —WAL, 211

In 1844, Thoreau climbed to the summit of Mount Greylock in the Berkshire Hills in Massachusetts, a view that overlooks the woodlands and villages of five states. He spent the entire night on the mountain, huddling against the wall of the Williams College observatory for warmth. In the morning he climbed the observatory's tower and found the landscape wrapped in a mist iridescent with the light of the rising sun.

I was up early and perched upon the top of this tower to see the daybreak. . . As the light increased, I discovered around me an ocean of mist, which by chance reached up exactly to the base of the tower, and shut out every vestige of the earth, while I was left floating on this fragment of the wreck of a world, on my carved plank, in cloudland; a situation which required no aid from the imagination to render it impressive. As the light in the east steadily increased, it revealed to me more clearly the new world into which I had risen in the night, the new *terra firma* perchance of my future life. There was not a crevice left through which the trivial places we name Massachusetts or Vermont or New York could be seen, while I still inhaled the clear atmosphere of a July morning—if it were July there. All around beneath me was spread for a hundred miles on every side, as far as the eye could reach, an undulating country of clouds, answering in the varied swell of its surface to the terrestrial world it veiled. It was such a country as we might see in dreams, with all the delights of paradise. . . . As there was wanting the symbol, so there was not the substance of impurity, no spot nor stain. It was a favor for which to be forever silent to be shown this vision. . . .

Here, as on earth, I saw the gracious god. . . . —WCM, 187–88

4

Sacred Nature

Thoreau was not a pantheist, unlike most transcendentalists, but believed that nature was the "face of God," as revelatory of the divine as sacred scripture. God could be found and experienced in nature, provided one approached the natural world with a pure mind and disciplined senses. For Thoreau, nature also revealed sacred depths lying within the human personality, the earth itself "spread out like a map" around him, he wrote, "the lining of my inmost soul exposed."

THE MANSIONS OF OUR FATHER'S HOUSE

I feel that I draw nearest to understanding the great secret of my life in my closest intercourse with nature. There is a reality and health in present nature, which is not to be found in any religion, and cannot be contemplated in antiquity. I suppose that what in other men is religion is in me love of nature. —PJ i, 55

These motions everywhere in nature must surely [be] the circulations of God. The flowing sail, the running stream, the waving tree, the roving wind—whence else their infinite health and freedom? I can see nothing so proper and holy as unrelaxed play and frolic in this bower God has built for us. The suspicion of sin never comes to this thought. —JOU i, 302

There is a depth in Autumn which no poetry has fathomed. Behind the rustling leaves, and the stacks of grain, and the bare clusters of the grape, I am sensible of a wholly new life which no man has lived. My faith is fed by the yellow leaf. Who can hear the wind in October rustling the wood without believing that this earth has more mysterious and nobler inhabitants than fauns and satyrs and fairies. In the fading hues of sunset, we see the portal to the other mansions of our Father's house. —PJ i, 51

Live in each season as it passes; breathe the air, drink the drink, taste the fruit, and resign yourself to the influences of each. . . . Be blown on by all the winds. Open all your pores and bathe in all the tides of nature, in all her streams and oceans, at all seasons. Miasma and infection are from within, not without. . . . Grow green with spring, yellow and ripe with autumn. Drink of each season's influence as a vial, a true panacea of all remedies mixed for your special use. . . . For all Nature is doing her best each moment to make us well. She exists for no other end. Do not resist her. —JOU v, 394–95

Nature always possesses a certain sonorousness, as in the hum of insects, the booming of ice, the crowing of cocks in the morning, and the barking of dogs in the night, which indicates her sound state. God's voice is but a clear bell sound. I drink in a wonderful health, a cordial, in sound. The effect of the slightest tinkling in the horizon measures my own soundness. I thank God for sound. . . . —JOU i, 227

The wonderful purity of nature at this season is a most pleasing fact. Every decayed stump and moss-grown stone and rail, and the dead leaves of autumn, are concealed by a clean napkin of snow. In the bare fields and tinkling woods, see what virtue survives. In the coldest and bleakest places, the warmest charities still maintain a foothold. A cold and searching wind drives away all contagion, and nothing can withstand it but what has a virtue in it, and accordingly, whatever we meet with in cold and bleak places, as the tops of mountains, we respect for a sort of sturdy innocence, a Puritan toughness. All things beside seem to be called in for shelter, and what stays out must be part of the original frame of the universe, and of such valor as God himself. It is invigorating to breathe the cleansed air. Its greater fineness and purity are visible to the eye, and we would fain stay out long and late, that the gales may sigh through us, too, as through the leafless trees, and fit us for the winter—as if we hoped so to borrow some pure and steadfast virtue, which will stead us in all seasons. —ESS, 30

Fishermen, hunters, woodchoppers, and others, spending their lives in the fields and woods, in a peculiar sense a part of Nature themselves, are often in a more favorable mood for observing her, in the intervals of their pursuits, than philosophers or poets even, who approach her with expectation. She is not afraid to exhibit herself to them. —WAL, 197

To anticipate, not the sunrise and the dawn merely, but, if possible, Nature herself! How many mornings, summer and winter, before yet any neighbor was stirring about his business, have I been about mine! No doubt, many of my townsmen have met me returning from this enterprise, farmers starting for Boston in the twilight, or woodchoppers going to their work. It is true, I never assisted the sun materially in his rising, but, doubt not, it was of the last importance only to be present at it.

So many autumn, ay, and winter days, spent outside the town, trying to hear what was in the wind, to hear and carry it express! I well-nigh sunk all my capital in it, and lost my own breath into the bargain, running in the face of it. . . .

For many years I was self-appointed inspector of snowstorms and rainstorms, and did my duty faithfully; surveyor, if not of highways, then of forest paths and all across-lot routes, keeping them open, and ravines bridged and passable at all seasons. . . .

—WAL, 15–16

ALL GOOD THINGS ARE WILD

Life consists with wildness. The most alive is the wildest. Not yet subdued to man, its presence refreshes him. One who pressed forward incessantly and never rested from his labors, who grew fast and made infinite demands on life, would always find himself in a new country or wilderness, and surrounded by the raw material of life. —ESS 163–64

I seem to see somewhat more of my own kith and kin in the lichens on the rocks than in any books. It does seem as if mine were a peculiarly wild nature, which so yearns toward all wildness. —JOU i, 296

The wilderness is near as well as dear to every man. Even the oldest villages are indebted to the border of wild wood which surrounds them, more than to the gardens of men. There is something indescribably inspiriting and beautiful in the aspect of the forest skirting and occasionally jutting into the midst of new towns, which, like the sand-heaps of fresh fox-burrows, have sprung up in their midst. The very uprightness of the pines and maples asserts the ancient rectitude and vigor of nature. Our lives need the relief of such a background, where the pine flourishes and the jay still screams. —WCM, 171

I found in myself, and still find, an instinct toward a higher, or, as it is named, spiritual life, as do most men, and another toward a primitive rank and savage one, and I reverence them both. I love the wild not less than the good. —WAL, 197

In short, all good things are wild and free. — ESS, 168

In literature it is only the wild that attracts us. Dullness is but another name for tameness. It is the uncivilized free and wild thinking in Hamlet and the Iliad, in all the scriptures and mythologies, not learned in the schools, that delights us. As the wild duck is more swift and beautiful than the tame, so is the wild—the mallard—thought, which 'mid falling dews wings its way above the fens. A truly good book is something as natural, and as unexpectedly and unaccountably fair and perfect, as a wild-flower discovered on the prairies of the West or in the jungles of the East. —ESS, 166

We can never have enough of Nature. We must be refreshed by the site of inexhaustible vigor . . . the wilderness with its living and its decaying trees, the thundercloud, and the rain which lasts three weeks and produces freshets. We need to witness our own limits transgressed, and some life pasturing freely where we never wander. . . . I love to see that Nature is so rife with life that myriads can be afforded to be sacrificed and suffered to prey on one another . . . tadpoles which herons gobble up, and tortoises and toads run over in the road. . . . With the liability to accident, we must see how little account is to be made of it. The impression made on a wise man is that of universal innocence. —WAL, 297

NO HIGHER HEAVEN

In proportion as I have celestial thoughts, is the necessity for me to be out and behold the western sky before sunset these winter days. That is the symbol of the unclouded mind that knows neither winter nor summer. What is your thought like? That is the hue, that the purity and transparency and distance from earthly taint of my innermost mind, for whatever we see without is a symbol of something within, and that which is farthest off is the symbol of what is deepest within. A lover of contemplation, accordingly, will gaze much into the sky. —JOU iii, 201

When Nature ceases to be supernatural to a man, what will he do then? Of what worth is human life, if its actions are no longer to have this sublime and unexplored scenery? Who will build a cottage and dwell in it with enthusiasm, if not in the Elysian fields? —PJ i, 481

Ah! I have penetrated to those meadows on the morning of many a first spring day, jumping from hummock to hummock, from willow root to willow root, when the wild river valley and the woods were bathed in so pure and bright a light as would have waked the dead, if they had been slumbering in their graves, as some suppose. There needs no stronger proof of immortality. All things must live in such a light. O Death, where was thy sting? O Grave, where was thy victory then? —WAL, 296–97

Men nowhere, east or west, live yet a *natural* life, round which the vine clings, and which the elm willingly shadows. Man would desecrate it by his touch, and so the beauty of the world remains veiled to him. He needs not only to be spiritualized, but *naturalized*, on the soil of earth. Who shall conceive what kind of roof the heavens might extend over him, what seasons minister to him, and what employment dignify his life! Only the convalescent raise the veil of nature. An immortality in his life would confer immortality on his abode. The winds should be his breath, the seasons his moods, and he should impart of his serenity to Nature herself. But such as we know him he is ephemeral like the scenery which surrounds him, and does not aspire to an enduring existence. . . .

We need pray for no higher heaven than the pure senses can furnish, a *purely* sensuous life. Our present senses are but the rudiments of what they are destined to become. We are comparatively deaf and dumb and blind, and without smell or taste or feeling. Every generation makes the discovery that its divine vigor has been dissipated, and each sense and faculty misapplied and debauched. The ears were made, not for such trivial uses as men are wont to suppose, but to hear celestial sounds. The eyes were not made for such groveling uses as they are now put to and worn out by, but to behold beauty now invisible. May we not *see* God? —WCM, 379–82

5

God, Religion, and Time

Religion for Thoreau was founded on experience, rather than belief, and constituted a search for an "infinite, all-absorbing divine" at the heart of a sacred natural world. In this sense, Thoreau may best be understood as a religious empiricist, relying upon his own experience of an ineffable, divine presence for confirmation of higher reality rather than through the received wisdom of scriptural authority. God was real for Thoreau, but was to be experienced in the present moment, and within, rather than after death in a heavenly kingdom. "Heaven is the inmost place," he wrote in 1841. "The good have not to travel far."

THE IDEAL AND THE ACTUAL

I believe that there is an ideal or real nature, infinitely more perfect than the actual, as there is an ideal life of man. Elsewhere are the glorious summers which envisioned sometimes visit my brain.

On one side of man is the actual, and on the other the ideal. The former is the province of the reason; it is even a divine light when directed upon it, but it cannot reach forward into the ideal without blindness. The moon was made to rule by night, but the sun to rule by day. Reason will be but a pale cloud, like the moon, when one ray of divine light comes to illumine the soul.

—JOU i, 359

Shams and delusions are esteemed for soundest truths, while reality is fabulous. If men would steadily observe realities only, and not allow themselves to be deluded, life, to compare it with such things as we know, would be like a fairy tale and the Arabian

Nights' entertainments. If we respected only what is inevitable and has a right to be, music and poetry would resound along the streets. When we are unhurried and wise, we perceive that only great and worthy things have any permanent and absolute existence, that petty fears and petty pleasures are but the shadow of the reality. This is always exhilarating and sublime. By closing the eyes and slumbering, and consenting to be deceived by shows, men establish and confirm their daily life of routine and habit everywhere, which still is built on purely illusory foundations. . . . I perceive that we inhabitants of New England live this mean life that we do because our vision does not penetrate the surface of things. We think that that *is* which *appears* to be. If a man should walk through this town and see only the reality, where, think you, would the "Mill-dam" go to? If he should give us an account of the realities he beheld there, we should not recognize the place in his description. Look at a meetinghouse, or a courthouse, or a jail, or a shop, or a dwellinghouse, and say what that thing really is before a true gaze, and they would all go to pieces in your account of them. — WAL, 90–91

The greatest gains and values are farthest from being appreciated. We easily come to doubt if they exist. We soon forget them. They are the highest reality. Perhaps the facts most astounding and most real are never communicated by man to man. The true harvest of my daily life is somewhat as intangible and indescribable as the tints of morning or evening. It is a little stardust caught, a segment of the rainbow which I have clutched. — WAL, 203

The anecdotes of modern astronomy affect me in the same way as do those faint revelations of the Real which are vouchsafed to men from time to time, or rather from eternity to eternity. When I remember the history of that faint light in our firmament which we call Venus, . . . how Copernicus, reasoning long and patiently about the matter, predicted confidently concerning it, before yet the telescope had been invented, that if ever men came to see it more clearly than they did then, they would discover that it had phases like our moon, and that within a century

after his death the telescope was invented, and that prediction verified, by Galileo—I am not without hope that we may, even here and now, obtain some accurate information concerning that OTHER WORLD which the instinct of mankind has so long predicted. . . . Why may not our speculations penetrate as far into the immaterial starry system, of which the former is but the outward and visible type? Surely, we are provided with senses as well fitted to penetrate the spaces of the real, the substantial, the eternal, as these outward are to penetrate the material universe.
—WCM, 385–87

THE DIVINE

Thoreau was eclectic in his conception of a divine godhead. Throughout his writings, he used dozens of names for God, ranging from the biblical—Father, the Almighty—to the naturalistic—Director of Lightning, Artist of the World, Great Spirit—to the transcendental—the Universal Soul, the Uncompromising Spirit, the Everlasting Something.

God prefers that you approach him thoughtful, not penitent, though you are the chief of sinners. It is only by forgetting yourself that you draw near to him. —JOU ii, 3

It seems to me that the god that is commonly worshipped in civilized countries is not at all divine, though he bears a divine name, but is the overwhelming authority and respectability of mankind combined. Men reverence one another, not yet God. —WCM, 65

The unconsciousness of man is the consciousness of God.
—WCM, 329

If Nature is our mother, is not God much more? God should come into our thoughts with no more parade than the zephyr into our ears. Only strangers approach him with ceremony. How rarely in our English tongue do we find expressed any affection for God! No sentiment is so rare as love of God—universal love.
—JOU i, 326

I am startled that God can make me so rich even with my own cheap stores. It needs but a few wisps of straw in the sun, or some small word dropped, or that has long lain silent in some book. When heaven begins and the dead arise, no trumpet is blown; perhaps the south wind will blow. What if you or I be dead! God is alive still. —JOU i, 328

The birds, the squirrels, the alders, the pines, they seem serene and in their places. I wonder if my life looks as serene to them too. Does no creature, then, see with the eyes of its own narrow destiny, but with God's? When God made man, he reserved some parts and some rights to himself. The eye has many qualities which belong to God more than man. It is his lightning which flashes in it. When I look into my companion's eye, I think it is God's private mine. It is a noble feature; it cannot be degraded, for God can look on all things undefiled. —JOU i, 331

While men believe in the infinite some ponds will be thought to be bottomless. —WAL, 269

The great God is very calm withal. How superfluous is any excitement in his creatures! He listens equally to the prayers of the believer and the unbeliever. The moods of man should unfold and alternate as gradually and placidly as those of nature. The sun shines for aye! —JOU i, 315

My life, my life! why will you linger? Are the years short and the months of no account? How often has long delay quenched my aspirations! Can God afford that I should forget him? Is he so indifferent to my career? Can heaven be postponed with no more ado? —JOU i, 327

RELIGION

While Thoreau is famous for his criticisms of institutionalized religions, he approached his life with what amounts to a religious, even quasi-monastic sensibility. It was not religions themselves or religious belief to which Thoreau took exception, but rather the unexamined acceptance of religious doctrine and ideology by men and women who "have their scheme of the universe all cut and dried." For Thoreau, ultimate truth was never a settled matter, but was to be rediscovered by each principled individual within a continuously unfolding divine creation.

Thoreau was also offended by the strident sectarianism of the Christian churches of the mid-nineteenth century, finding no basis for their claims of a divinely ordained exceptionalism. "The wisest man preaches no doctrines," he concluded in the "Sunday" section of A Week on the Concord and Merrimack Rivers, *"he has no scheme; he sees no rafter, not even a cobweb, against the heavens. It is clear sky."*

What is religion? That which is never spoken. —JOU xi, 113

I do not prefer one religion or philosophy to another. I have no sympathy with the bigotry and ignorance which make transient and partial and puerile distinctions between one man's faith or form of faith and another's—as Christian and heathen. I pray to be delivered from narrowness, partiality, exaggeration, bigotry. To the philosophers, all sects, all nations are alike. I like Brahman, the Great Spirit, . . . as well as God. —JOU ii, 4

For my part if I have any creed it is so to live as to preserve and increase the susceptibleness of my nature to noble impulses—first to observe if any light shine on me and then faithfully to follow it. . . .

The strains of a more heroic faith vibrate through the week days and the fields than through the Sabbath and the Church. To shut the ears to the immediate voice of God, and prefer to know him by report will be the only sin. —Letter to Isiah T. Williams, COR, 52

Moreover, with wisdom we shall learn liberality. The solitary hired man on a farm in the outskirts of Concord, who has had his second birth and peculiar religious experience, and is driven as he believes into the silent gravity and exclusiveness by his faith, may think it is not true; but Zoroaster, thousands of years ago, travelled the same road and had the same experience; but he, being wise, knew it to be universal, and treated his neighbors accordingly, and is even said to have invented and established worship among men. Let him humbly commune with Zoroaster then, and through the liberalizing influence of all the worthies, with Jesus Christ himself, and let "our church" go by the board. —WAL, 102

Most people with whom I talk, men and women even of some originality and genius, have their scheme of the universe all cut and dried—very *dry*, I assure you, to hear, dry enough to burn, dry-rotted and powder-post, methinks. . . . Some, to me, seemingly very unimportant and unsubstantial things and relations, are for them everlastingly settled—as Father, Son, and Holy Ghost, and the like. These are like the everlasting hills to them. But in all my wanderings I never came across the least vestige of authority for these things. They have not left so distinct a trace as the delicate flower of a remote geological period on the coal in my grate. The wisest man preaches no doctrines; he has no scheme; he sees no rafter, not even a cobweb, against the heavens. It is clear sky. —WCM, 69–70

Those who have no knowledge of the divine appoint themselves defenders of the divine, as champions of the church, etc. I have been astonished to observe how long some audiences can endure to hear a man speak on a subject which he knows nothing about, as religion for instance. . . . —JOU ii, 404

THE EAST

Thoreau first encountered Indian contemplative texts in his early twenties, while living with Ralph Waldo Emerson, whose library housed the largest collection of Eastern philosophy in America. He found confirmation in them of the sacred character of his own ineffable experiences, and an affirmation of the contemplative life to which he had been drawn since his youth. While at Walden, Thoreau made a close study of the Bhagavad Gita, *and was inspired by his reading of the* Upanishads *in the early 1850s. The origins of America's enchantment with Eastern, and especially Indian, spirituality can be traced to the writings of both Emerson and Thoreau.*

Ex oriente lux may still be the motto of scholars, for though Greece and Rome politically have passed away, that source of light is not yet exhausted. The Western world has not yet derived from the East all the light which it is destined to receive.

—WCM, 143

In the morning I bathe my intellect in the stupendous and cosmogonal philosophy of the Bhagavad Gita, since whose composition years of the gods have elapsed, and in comparison with which our modern world and its literature seem puny and trivial; and I doubt if that philosophy is not to be referred to a previous state of existence, so remote is its sublimity from our conceptions. . . . —WAL, 279

"Wherefore, O Arjuna, resolve to fight," is the advice of the god to the irresolute soldier who fears to slay his best friends. It is a sublime conservatism; as wide as the world, and as unwearied as time. . . . The end is an immense consolation; eternal absorption in Brahman (God). . . .

Arabia—Persia—Hindustan—are the native land of contemplation. —JOU i, 243

The Hindus are more serenely and thoughtfully religious than the Hebrews. [The Indian] religious books describe the first inquisitive and contemplative access to God. —JOU ii, 3

The impression which those sublime Sentences [from the laws of Manu] made on me last night has awakened me before any cockcrowing. Their influence lingers around me like a fragrance, or as the fog hangs over the earth late into the day.

The very locusts and crickets of a summer day are but later or older glosses on the Dharma Sastra of the Hindus, a continuation of the sacred code. —JOU i, 267

In the Hindu scripture the idea of man is quite illimitable and sublime. There is nowhere a loftier conception of his destiny. He is at length lost in Brahma himself, "the divine male." Indeed, the distinction of races in this life is only the commencement of a series of degrees which ends in Brahma.

The veneration in which the Vedas are held is itself a remarkable fact. Their code embraced the whole moral life of the Hindu, and in such a case there is no other truth than sincerity. . . .

In inquiring into the origin and genuineness of this scripture it is impossible to tell when the divine agency in its composition ceased, and the human began. . . .

There is no grander conception of creation anywhere. It is peaceful as a dream, and so is the annihilation of the world. It is such a beginning and ending as the morning and evening, for they had learned that God's methods are not violent. It was such an awakening as might have been heralded by the faint dreaming chirp of the crickets before the dawn.

The very indistinctness of its theogony implies a sublime truth. . . . The divinity is so fleeting that its attributes are never expressed. —JOU i, 275–76

The sublime sentences of [the Laws of] Manu carry us back to a time when purification and sacrifice and self-devotion had a place in the faith of men, and were not as now a superstition. They contain a subtle and refined philosophy also, such as in these times is not accompanied with so lofty and pure a devotion.

—JOU i, 280

The New Testament is remarkable for its pure morality; the best of the Hindu Scripture, for its pure intellectuality. The reader is nowhere raised into and sustained in a higher, purer, or *rarer* region of thought than in the *Bhagavad Gita*. —WCM, 13

In comparison with the philosophers of the East, we may say that modern Europe has yet given birth to none. Beside the vast and cosmogonal philosophy of the *Bhagavad Gita*, even our Shakespeare seems sometimes youthfully green and practical merely. Some of these sublime sentences, as the Chaldaean oracles of Zoroaster, still surviving after a thousand revolutions and translations, alone make us doubt if the poetic form and dress are not transitory, and not essential to the most effective and enduring expression of thought. —WCM, 143

Christianity, on the other hand, is humane, practical, and, in a large sense, radical. So many years and ages of the gods those Eastern sages sat contemplating Brahma, uttering in silence the mystic "Om," being absorbed into the essence of the Supreme Being, never going out of themselves, but subsiding farther and deeper within; so infinitely wise, yet infinitely stagnant; until, at last, in that same Asia, but in the western part of it, appeared a youth, wholly unforetold by them. . . . Christ is the prince of Reformers and Radicals. Many expressions in the New Testament come naturally to the lips of all Protestants, and it furnishes the most pregnant and practical texts. There is no harmless dreaming, no wise speculation in it, but everywhere a substratum of good sense. It never *reflects*, but it *repents*. There is no poetry in it, we may say, nothing regarded in the light of beauty merely, but moral truth is its object. All mortals are convicted by its conscience. —WCM, 136–37

GOD CULMINATES IN THE PRESENT MOMENT

In any weather, at any hour of the day or night, I have been anxious to improve the nick of time, and notch it on my stick too; to stand on the meeting of two eternities, the past and future, which is precisely the present moment; to toe that line. —WAL, 14

Above all, we cannot afford not to live in the present. He is blessed over all mortals who loses no moment of the passing life in remembering the past. Unless our philosophy hears the cock crow in every barnyard within our horizon, it is belated. That sound commonly reminds us that we are growing rusty and antique in our employments and habits of thoughts. His philosophy comes down to a more recent time than ours. There is something suggested by it that is a newer testament—the gospel according to this moment. He has not fallen astern; he has got up early and kept up early, and to be where he is is to be in season, in the foremost rank of time. It is an expression of the health and soundness of Nature, a brag for all the world—healthiness as of a spring burst forth, a new fountain of the Muses, to celebrate this last instant of time. Where he lives no fugitive slave laws are passed. Who has not betrayed his master many times since last he heard that note? —ESS, 176

In eternity there is indeed something true and sublime. But all these times and places and occasions are now and here. God himself culminates in the present moment, and will never be more divine in the lapse of all the ages. And we are enabled to apprehend at all what is sublime and noble only by the perpetual instilling and drenching of the reality that surrounds us. The universe constantly and obediently answers to our conceptions; whether we travel fast or slow, the track is laid for us. Let us spend our lives in conceiving then. The poet or the artist never yet had so fair and noble a design but some of his posterity at least could accomplish it. —WAL, 91

We should be blessed if we lived in the present always, and took advantage of every accident that befell us, . . . and did not spend our time in atoning for the neglect of past opportunities, which we call doing our duty. We loiter in winter while it is already spring. In a pleasant spring morning, all men's sins are forgiven. —WAL, 294

I must live above all in the present. —JOU ii, 138

There is a season for everything, and we do not notice a given phenomenon except at that season, if, indeed, it can be called the same phenomenon any other season. . . . A wise man will know what game to play today and play it. We must not be governed by rigid rules, as by the almanac, but let the season rule us. . . . Nothing must be postponed. Take time by the forelock. Now or never! You must live in the present, launch yourself on every wave, find your eternity in each moment. . . . There is no world for the penitent and regretful. —JOU xii, 159–60

NATURE NEVER MAKES HASTE

Why should we live with such hurry and waste of life? We are determined to be starved before we are hungry. Men say that a stitch in time saves nine, and so they take a thousand stitches today to save nine tomorrow. —WAL, 87

Nature never makes haste; her systems revolve at an even pace. The bud swells imperceptibly, without hurry or confusion, as though the short spring days were an eternity. All her operations seem separately, for the time, the single object for which all things tarry. Why, then, should man hasten as if anything less than eternity were allotted for the least deed? Let him consume never so many aeons, so that he go about the meanest task well, though it be but the paring of his nails. If the setting sun seems to hurry him to improve the day while it lasts, the chant of the crickets fails not to reassure him, even-measured as of old, teaching him to take his own time henceforth forever. The wise man is restful, never restless or impatient. He each moment abides there where he is, as some walkers actually rest the whole body at each step, while others never relax the muscles of the leg till the accumulated fatigue obliges them to stop short.

As the wise is not anxious that time wait for him, neither does he wait for it. —JOU i, 92

Time is but the stream I go a-fishing in. I drink at it; but while I drink I see the sandy bottom and detect how shallow it is. Its thin current slides away, but eternity remains. I would drink deeper; fish in the sky, whose bottom is pebbly with stars. I cannot count one. I know not the first letter of the alphabet. I have always been regretting that I was not as wise as the day I was born. The intellect is a cleaver; it discerns and rifts its way into the secret of things. I do not wish to be any more busy with my hands than is necessary. My head is hands and feet. I feel all my best faculties concentrated in it. My instinct tells me that my head is an organ for burrowing, as some creatures use their snout and forepaws, and with it I would mine and burrow my way through these hills. I think that the richest vein is somewhere hereabouts; so by the divining rod and thin rising vapors I judge; and here I will begin to mine. —WAL, 92

When I visit again some haunt of my youth, I am glad to find that nature wears so well. The landscape is indeed something real, and solid, and sincere, and I have not put my foot through it yet. There is a pleasant tract on the bank of the Concord, called Conantum, which I have in my mind—the old deserted farm-house, the desolate pasture with its bleak cliff, the open wood, the river-reach, the green meadow in the midst, and the moss-grown wild-apple orchard—places where one may have many thoughts and not decide anything. It is a scene which I can not only remember, as I might a vision, but when I will can bodily revisit, and find it even so, unaccountable, yet unpretending in its pleasant dreariness. When my thoughts are sensible of change, I love to see and sit on rocks which I *have* known, and pry into their moss, and see unchangeableness so established. I not yet gray on rocks forever gray, I no longer green under the ever-greens. There is something even in the lapse of time by which time recovers itself. —WCM, 350–51

THE LAW OF THEIR DEATH IS THE LAW OF NEW LIFE

Every part of nature teaches that the passing away of one life is the making room for another. The oak dies down to the ground, leaving within its rind a rich virgin mould, which will impart a vigorous life to an infant forest. The pine leaves a sandy and sterile soil, the harder woods a strong and fruitful mould.

So this constant abrasion and decay makes the soil of my future growth. As I live now so shall I reap. If I grow pines and birches, my virgin mould will not sustain the oak; but pines and birches, or, perchance, weeds and brambles, will constitute my second growth. —JOU i, 3–4

Thoreau's brother, John, died of lockjaw on January 11, 1842, followed shortly by the death of six-year-old Waldo Emerson from scarlet fever. Thoreau was profoundly shocked by their deaths, suffering an extended emotional depression and sympathetically experiencing the symptoms of lockjaw. Yet he was capable of viewing death with an almost otherworldly detachment, as is evident below in two letters of consolation he wrote to Emerson and Emerson's disabled sister, Lucy Brown, written in the midst of his own profound grieving.

March 2, 1842

Dear friend,

I believe I have nothing new to tell you, for what was news you have learned from other sources. I am much the same person that I was. . . .

Soon after John's death I listened to a music box, and if, at any time, that even had seemed inconsistent with the beauty and harmony of the universe, it was then gently constrained into the placid course of nature by those steady notes. . . .

Only nature has a right to grieve perpetually, for she only is innocent. Soon the ice will melt, and the blackbirds sing along the river which he [John] frequented, as pleasantly as ever. The same everlasting serenity will appear in this face of God, and we will not be sorrowful, if he is not.

I do not wish to see John ever again—I mean him who is dead—but that other whom only he would have wished to see, or to be, of whom he was the imperfect representative. For we are not what we are, nor do we treat or esteem each other for such, but for what we are capable of being.

As for Waldo, he died as the mist rises from the brook, which the sun will soon dart his rays through. Do not the flowers die every autumn? He had not even taken root here. . . . Neither will nature manifest any sorrow at his death, but soon the note of the lark will be heard down in the meadow, and fresh dandelions will spring from the old stocks where he plucked them last summer. . . .

—Letter to Lucy Brown, COR, 62–63

March 11, 1842

Dear Friend

Nature is not ruffled by the rudest blast. The hurricane only snaps a few twigs in some nook of the forest. The snow attains its average depth each winter, and the chickadee lisps the same notes. The old laws prevail in spite of pestilence and famine. No genius or virtue so rare and revolutionary appears in town or village, that the pine ceases to exude resin in the wood, or beast or bird lays aside its habits.

How plain that death is only the phenomenon of the individual or class. Nature does not recognize it, she finds her own again under new forms without loss. Yet death is beautiful when seen to be a law, and not an accident—It is as common as life. . . .

Every blade in the fields every leaf in the forest, lays down his life in its season as beautifully as it was taken up. . . . Dead trees—sere leaves—dried grass and herbs—are not these a good part of our life? . . .

When we look over the field, we are not saddened because the particular flowers or grasses will wither—for the law of their death is the law of new life. . . .

So it is with the human plant. We are partial and selfish when we lament the death of the individual, unless our plaint be a paean to the departed soul, and a sigh as the wind sighs over the fields, which no shrub interprets into its private grief.

One might as well go into mourning for every sere leaf—but the more innocent and wiser soul will snuff a fragrance in the gales of autumn, and congratulate Nature upon her health.

—Letter to Emerson, COR, 64–65

The sad memory of departed friends is soon incrusted over with sublime and pleasing thoughts, as their monuments are overgrown with moss. Nature doth thus kindly heal every wound. By the mediation of a thousand little mosses and fungi, the most unsightly objects become radiant of beauty. There seem to be two sides to this world, presented us at different times, as we see things in growth or dissolution, in life or death. For seen with the eye of a poet, as God sees them, all are alive and beautiful; but seen with the historical eye, or the eye of the memory, they are dead and offensive. If we see Nature as pausing, immediately all mortifies and decays; but seen as progressing, she is beautiful.

—JOU i, 328

Thoreau's father died on February 3, 1859, following a lengthy illness. Thoreau nursed him through much of this period, prompting his mother to remark that "But for this I should never have seen the tender side of Henry, who had nursed him with loving care."

I have touched a body which was flexible and warm, yet tenantless—warmed by what fire? When the spirit that animated some matter has left it, who else, what else, can animate it? . . .

I perceive that we partially die ourselves through sympathy at the death of each of our friends or near relatives. Each such experience is an assault on our vital force. It becomes a source of wonder that they who have lost many friends still live. After long watching around the sickbed of a friend, we, too, partially give up the ghost with him, and are less to be identified with this state of things.

—JOU xi, 435–38

6

Essays

LIFE WITHOUT PRINCIPLE

The source material for this essay was first delivered as a lecture in Providence, Rhode Island, on December 6, 1854, as "What Shall It Profit?" Thoreau repeated the lecture over the next few years, and edited it for publication during the final months of his life. It was published under the current title in The Atlantic Monthly, *October 1863.*

At a lyceum, not long since, I felt that the lecturer had chosen a theme too foreign to himself, and so failed to interest me as much as he might have done. He described things not in or near to his heart, but toward his extremities and superficies. There was, in this sense, no truly central or centralizing thought in the lecture. I would have had him deal with his privatest experience, as the poet does. . . .

So now I would say something similar to you, my readers. Since *you* are my readers, and I have not been much of a traveller, I will not talk about people a thousand miles off, but come as near home as I can. As the time is short, I will leave out all the flattery, and retain all the criticism.

Let us consider the way in which we spend our lives.

This world is a place of business. What an infinite bustle! I am awaked almost every night by the panting of the locomotive. It interrupts my dreams. There is no sabbath. It would be glorious to see mankind at leisure for once. It is nothing but work, work,

work. I cannot easily buy a blank-book to write thoughts in; they are commonly ruled for dollars and cents. An Irishman, seeing me making a minute in the fields, took it for granted that I was calculating my wages. If a man was tossed out of a window when an infant, and so made a cripple for life, or scared out of his wits by the Indians, it is regretted chiefly because he was thus incapacitated for—business! I think that there is nothing, not even crime, more opposed to poetry, to philosophy, ay, to life itself, than this incessant business. . . .

If a man walk in the woods for love of them half of each day, he is in danger of being regarded as a loafer; but if he spends his whole day as a speculator, shearing off those woods and making earth bald before her time, he is esteemed an industrious and enterprising citizen. As if a town had no interest in its forests but to cut them down! . . .

The ways by which you may get money almost without exception lead downward. To have done anything by which you earned money *merely* is to have been truly idle or worse. If the laborer gets no more than the wages which his employer pays him, he is cheated, he cheats himself. If you would get money as a writer or lecturer, you must be popular, which is to go down perpendicularly. Those services which the community will most readily pay for, it is most disagreeable to render. You are paid for being something less than a man. The state does not commonly reward a genius any more wisely. Even the poet laureate would rather not have to celebrate the accidents of royalty. He must be bribed with a pipe of wine; and perhaps another poet is called away from his muse to gauge that very pipe. As for my own business, even that kind of surveying which I could do with most satisfaction my employers do not want. They would prefer that I should do my work coarsely and not too well, ay, not well enough. When I observe that there are different ways of surveying, my employer commonly asks which will give him the most land, not which is most correct. I once invented a rule for measuring cord-wood, and tried to introduce it in Boston; but the measurer there told me that the sellers did not wish to have their wood measured correctly—that he was already too accurate for them, and therefore they commonly got their wood measured in Charlestown before crossing the bridge.

The aim of the laborer should be, not to get his living, to get "a good job," but to perform well a certain work; and, even in a pecuniary sense, it would be economy for a town to pay its laborers so well that they would not feel that they were working for low ends, as for a livelihood merely, but for scientific, or even moral ends. Do not hire a man who does your work for money, but him who does it for love of it. . . .

The community has no bribe that will tempt a wise man. You may raise money enough to tunnel a mountain, but you cannot raise money enough to hire a man who is minding *his own* business. An efficient and valuable man does what he can, whether the community pay him for it or not. The inefficient offer their inefficiency to the highest bidder, and are forever expecting to be put into office. One would suppose that they were rarely disappointed.

Perhaps I am more than usually jealous with respect to my freedom. I feel that my connection with and obligation to society are still very slight and transient. Those slight labors which afford me a livelihood, and by which it is allowed that I am to some extent serviceable to my contemporaries, are as yet commonly a pleasure to me, and I am not often reminded that they are a necessity. So far I am successful. But I foresee that if my wants should be much increased, the labor required to supply them would become a drudgery. If I should sell both my forenoons and afternoons to society, as most appear to do, I am sure that for me there would be nothing left worth living for. I trust that I shall never thus sell my birthright for a mess of pottage. I wish to suggest that a man may be very industrious, and yet not spend his time well. There is no more fatal blunderer than he who consumes the greater part of his life getting his living. All great enterprises are self-supporting. The poet, for instance, must sustain his body by his poetry, as a steam planing-mill feeds its boilers with the shavings it makes. You must get your living by loving. But as it is said of the merchants that ninety-seven in a hundred fail, so the life of men generally, tried by this standard, is a failure, and bankruptcy may be surely prophesied. . . .

It is remarkable that there is little or nothing to be remembered written on the subject of getting a living; how to make getting a living not merely honest and honorable, but altogether inviting and glorious; for if *getting* a living is not so, then living is not. One would think, from looking at literature, that this question had never disturbed a solitary individual's musings. Is it that men are too much disgusted with their experience to speak of it. . . .

The title *wise* is, for the most part, falsely applied. How can one be a wise man, if he does not know any better how to live than other men?—if he is only more cunning and intellectually subtle? Does Wisdom work in a tread-mill? or does she teach how to succeed *by her example?* Is there any such thing as wisdom not applied to life? Is she merely the miller who grinds the finest logic? It is pertinent to ask if Plato got his *living* in a better way or more successfully than his contemporaries—or did he succumb to the difficulties of life like other men? Did he seem to prevail over some of them merely by indifference, or by assuming grand airs? or find it easier to live, because his aunt remembered him in her will? The ways in which most men get their living, that is, live, are mere makeshifts, and a shirking of the real business of life—chiefly because they do not know, but partly because they do not mean, any better.

The rush to California, for instance, and the attitude, not merely of merchants, but of philosophers and prophets, so called, in relation to it, reflect the greatest disgrace on mankind. That so many are ready to live by luck, and so get the means of commanding the labor of others less lucky, without contributing any value to society! And that is called enterprise! I know of no more startling development of the immorality of trade, and all the common modes of getting a living. The philosophy and poetry and religion of such a mankind are not worth the dust of a puffball. The hog that gets his living by rooting, stirring up the soil so, would be ashamed of such company. If I could command the wealth of all the worlds by lifting my finger, I would not pay *such* a price for it. . . .

I was thinking, accidentally, of my own unsatisfactory life, doing as others do; and with that vision of the diggings still before me, I asked myself why *I* might not be washing some gold daily, though it were only the finest particles—why *I* might not sink a shaft down to the gold within me, and work that mine. . . . At any rate, I might pursue some path, however solitary and narrow and crooked, in which I could walk with love and reverence. Wherever a man separates from the multitude, and goes his own way in this mood, there indeed is a fork in the road, though ordinary travelers may see only a gap in the paling. His solitary path across lots will turn out the *higher way* of the two. . . .

It is remarkable that among all the preachers there are so few moral teachers. The prophets are employed in excusing the ways of men. Most reverend seniors, the *illuminati* of the age, tell me, with a gracious, reminiscent smile, betwixt an aspiration and a shudder, not to be too tender about these things—to lump all that, that is, make a lump of gold of it. The highest advice I have heard on these subjects was groveling. The burden of it was—It is not worth your while to undertake to reform the world in this particular. Do not ask how your bread is buttered; it will make you sick, if you do—and the like. A man had better starve at once than lose his innocence in the process of getting his bread. If within the sophisticated man there is not an unsophisticated one, then he is but one of the devil's angels. As we grow old, we live more coarsely, we relax a little in our disciplines, and, to some extent, cease to obey our finest instincts. But we should be fastidious to the extreme of sanity, disregarding the gibes of those who are more unfortunate than ourselves. . . .

I hardly know an *intellectual* man, even, who is so broad and truly liberal that you can think aloud in his society. Most with whom you endeavor to talk soon come to a stand against some institution in which they appear to hold stock—that is, some particular, not universal, way of viewing things. They will continually thrust their own low roof, with its narrow skylight, between you and the sky, when it is the unobstructed heavens you would view. Get out of the way with your cobwebs; wash your windows, I say! In some lyceums they tell me that they have voted to exclude the subject of religion. But how do I know what their religion is, and when I am near to or far from it? I have walked into such an arena and done my best to make a clean breast of what religion I have experienced, and the audience never suspected what I was about. The lecture was as harmless as moonshine to them. Whereas, if I had read to them the biography of the greatest scamps in history, they might have thought that I had written the lives of the deacons of their church. Ordinarily, the inquiry is, Where did you come from? or, Where are you going? That was a more pertinent question which I overheard one of my auditors put to another once—"What does he lecture for?" It made me quake in my shoes.

To speak impartially, the best men that I know are not serene, a world in themselves. For the most part, they dwell in forms, and flatter and study effect only more finely than the rest. We select granite for the underpinning of our houses and barns; we build fences of stone; but we do not ourselves rest on an underpinning of granitic truth, the lowest primitive rock. Our sills are rotten. What stuff is the man made of who is not coexistent in our thought with the purest and subtilest truth? I often accuse my finest acquaintances of an immense frivolity; for, while there are manners and compliments we do not meet, we do not teach one another the lessons of honesty and sincerity that the brutes do, or of steadiness and solidity that the rocks do. The fault is commonly mutual, however; for we do not habitually demand any more of each other. . . .

Just so hollow and ineffectual, for the most part, is our ordinary conversation. Surface meets surface. When our life ceases to be inward and private, conversation degenerates into mere gossip. We rarely meet a man who can tell us any news which he has not read in a newspaper, or been told by his neighbor; and, for the most part, the only difference between us and our fellow is that he has seen the newspaper, or been out to tea, and we have not. In proportion as our inward life fails, we go more constantly and desperately to the post office. You may depend on it, that the poor fellow who walks away with the greatest number of letters, proud of his extensive correspondence, has not heard from himself this long while.

I do not know but it is too much to read one newspaper a week. I have tried it recently, and for so long it seems to me that I have not dwelt in my native region. The sun, the clouds, the snow, the trees say not so much to me. You cannot serve two masters. It requires more than a day's devotion to know and to possess the wealth of a day. . . .

All summer, and far into the autumn, perchance, you unconsciously went by the newspapers and the news, and now you find it was because the morning and the evening were full of news to you. Your walks were full of incidents. You attended, not to the affairs of Europe, but to your own affairs in Massachusetts fields. If you chance to live and move and have your being in that thin stratum in which the events that make the news transpire—thinner than the paper on which it is printed—then these things will fill the world for you; but if you soar above or dive below that plane, you cannot remember nor be reminded of them. Really to see the sun rise or go down every day, so to relate ourselves to a universal fact, would preserve us sane forever. Nations! What are nations? Tartars, and Huns, and Chinamen! Like insects, they swarm. The historian strives in vain to make them memorable. It is for want of a man that there are so many men. It is individuals that populate the world. . . .

Not without a slight shudder at the danger, I often perceive how near I had come to admitting into my mind the details of some trivial affair—the news of the street; and I am astonished to observe how willing men are to lumber their minds with such rubbish—to permit idle rumors and incidents of the most insignificant kind to intrude on ground which should be sacred to thought. Shall the mind be a public arena, where the affairs of the street and the gossip of the tea-table chiefly are discussed? Or shall it be a quarter of heaven itself—an hypæthral temple, consecrated to the service of the gods? I find it so difficult to dispose of the few facts which to me are significant, that I hesitate to burden my attention with those which are insignificant, which only a divine mind could illustrate. Such is, for the most part, the news in newspapers and conversation. It is important to preserve the mind's chastity in this respect. Think of admitting the details of a single case of the criminal court into our thoughts, to stalk profanely through their very *sanctum sanctorum* for an hour, ay for many hours! to make a barroom of the mind's inmost apartment, as if for so long the dust of the street had occupied us—the very street itself, with all its travel, its bustle, and filth, had passed through our thoughts' shrine! Would it not be an intellectual and moral suicide . . .?

By all kinds of traps and signboards, threatening the extreme penalty of the divine law, exclude such trespassers from the only ground which can be sacred to you. It is so hard to forget what it is worse than useless to remember! If I am to be a thoroughfare, I prefer that it be of the mountain brooks, the Parnassian streams, and not the town sewers. There is inspiration, that gossip which comes to the ear of the attentive mind from the courts of heaven. There is the profane and stale revelation of the barroom and the police court. The same ear is fitted to receive both communications. Only the character of the hearer determines to which it shall be open, and to which closed. I believe that the mind can be permanently profaned by the habit of attending to trivial things, so that all our thoughts shall be tinged with triviality. . . .

If we have thus desecrated ourselves—as who has not?—the remedy will be by wariness and devotion to reconsecrate ourselves, and make once more a fane of the mind. We should treat our minds, that is, ourselves, as innocent and ingenuous children, whose guardians we are, and be careful what objects and what subjects we thrust on their attention. Read not the Times. Read the Eternities. Conventionalities are at length as had as impurities. Even the facts of science may dust the mind by their dryness, unless they are in a sense effaced each morning, or rather rendered fertile by the dews of fresh and living truth. Knowledge does not come to us by details, but in flashes of light from heaven. Yes, every thought that passes through the mind helps to wear and tear it, and to deepen the ruts, which, as in the streets of Pompeii, evince how much it has been used. How many things there are concerning which we might well deliberate whether we had better know them—had better let their peddling-carts be driven, even at the slowest trot or walk, over that bridge of glorious span by which we trust to pass at last from the farthest brink of time to the nearest shore of eternity! Have we no culture, no refinement—but skill only to live coarsely and serve the Devil?—to acquire a little worldly wealth, or fame, or liberty, and make a false show with it, as if we were all husk and shell, with no tender and living kernel to us? Shall our institutions be like those chestnut burs which contain abortive nuts, perfect only to prick the fingers?

America is said to be the arena on which the battle of freedom is to be fought; but surely it cannot be freedom in a merely political sense that is meant. Even if we grant that the American has freed himself from a political tyrant, he is still the slave of an economical and moral tyrant. Now that the republic—the *res-publica*—has been settled, it is time to look after the *res-privata*—the private state—to see, as the Roman senate charged its consuls, "ne quid res-PRIVATA *detrimenti caperet*," that the *private* state receive no detriment.

Do we call this the land of the free? What is it to be free from King George and continue the slaves of King Prejudice? What is it to be born free and not to live free? What is the value of any political freedom, but as a means to moral freedom? Is it a freedom to be slaves, or a freedom to be free, of which we boast? We are a nation of politicians, concerned about the outmost defenses only of freedom. It is our children's children who may perchance be really free. We tax ourselves unjustly. There is a part of us which is not represented. It is taxation without representation. We quarter troops, we quarter fools and cattle of all sorts upon ourselves. We quarter our gross bodies on our poor souls, till the former eat up all the latter's substance.

With respect to a true culture and manhood, we are essentially provincial still, not metropolitan—mere Jonathans. We are provincial, because we do not find at home our standards; because we do not worship truth, but the reflection of truth; because we are warped and narrowed by an exclusive devotion to trade and commerce and manufactures and agriculture and the like, which are but means, and not the end. . . .

When we want culture more than potatoes, and illumination more than sugar-plums, then the great resources of a world are taxed and drawn out, and the result, or staple production, is, not slaves, nor operatives, but men—those rare fruits called heroes, saints, poets, philosophers, and redeemers.

In short, as a snow-drift is formed where there is a lull in the wind, so, one would say, where there is a lull of truth, an institution springs up. But the truth blows right on over it, nevertheless, and at length blows it down.

What is called politics is comparatively something so superficial and inhuman, that practically, I have never fairly recognized that it concerns me at all. The newspapers, I perceive, devote some of their columns specially to politics or government without charge; and this, one would say, is all that saves it; but as I love literature and to some extent the truth also, I never read those columns at any rate. I do not wish to blunt my sense of right so much. I have not got to answer for having read a single President's Message. A strange age of the world this, when empires, kingdoms, and republics come a-begging to a private man's door, and utter their complaints at his elbow! I cannot take up a newspaper but I find that some wretched government or other, hard pushed and on its last legs, is interceding with me, the reader, to vote for it—more importunate than an Italian beggar; and if I have a mind to look at its certificate, made, perchance, by some benevolent merchant's clerk, or the skipper that brought it over, for it cannot speak a word of English itself, I shall probably read of the eruption of some Vesuvius, or the overflowing of some Po, true or forged, which brought it into this condition. I do not hesitate, in such a case, to suggest work, or the almshouse; or why not keep its castle in silence, as I do commonly? The poor President, what with preserving his popularity and doing his duty, is completely bewildered. The newspapers are the ruling power. Any other government is reduced to a few marines at Fort Independence. If a man neglects to read the *Daily Times*, government will go down on its knees to him, for this is the only treason in these days.

Those things which now most engage the attention of men, as politics and the daily routine, are, it is true, vital functions of human society, but should be unconsciously performed, like the corresponding functions of the physical body. They are *infra*-human, a kind of vegetation. I sometimes awake to a half-consciousness of them going on about me, as a man may become conscious of some of the processes of digestion in a morbid state, and so have the dyspepsia, as it is called. It is as if a thinker submitted himself to be rasped by the great gizzard of creation. Politics is, as it were, the gizzard of society, full of grit and gravel, and the two political parties are its two opposite halves—sometimes split into quarters, it may be, which grind on each other. Not only individuals, but states, have thus a confirmed dyspepsia, which expresses itself, you can imagine by what sort of eloquence. Thus our life is not altogether a forgetting, but also, alas! to a great extent, a remembering, of that which we should never have been conscious of, certainly not in our waking hours. Why should we not meet, not always as dyspeptics, to tell our bad dreams, but sometimes as *eu*peptics, to congratulate each other on the ever-glorious morning? I do not make an exorbitant demand, surely.

CIVIL DISOBEDIENCE

Thoreau's most celebrated and influential essay, "Civil Disobedience" originated as a lecture delivered on January 26, 1848, at the Concord Lyceum in response to the many questions he received about why he chose to go to jail in 1846 rather than pay a poll tax. Thoreau published the lecture as "Resistance to Civil Government" in 1849. Following his death, the essay was published in 1866 as "Civil Disobedience" and influenced Mahatma Gandhi and later Martin Luther King Jr. in their nonviolent struggles against colonialism and racism.

I heartily accept the motto— "That government is best which governs least"; and I should like to see it acted up to more rapidly and systematically. Carried out, it finally amounts to this, which also I believe—"That government is best which governs not at all"; and when men are prepared for it, that will be the kind of government which they will have. Government is at best but an expedient; but most governments are usually, and all governments are sometimes, inexpedient. The objections which have been brought against a standing army, and they are many and weighty, and deserve to prevail, may also at last be brought against a standing government. The standing army is only an arm of the standing government. The government itself, which is only the mode which the people have chosen to execute their will, is equally liable to be abused and perverted before the people can act through it. Witness the present Mexican war, the work of comparatively a few individuals using the standing government as their tool; for, in the outset, the people would not have consented to this measure.

This American government—what is it but a tradition, though a recent one, endeavoring to transmit itself unimpaired to posterity, but each instant losing some of its integrity? It has not the vitality and force of a single living man; for a single man can bend it to his will. It is a sort of wooden gun to the people themselves. But it is not the less necessary for this; for the people must have some complicated machinery or other, and hear its din, to satisfy that idea of government which they have. Governments show thus how successfully men can be imposed on, even impose on themselves, for their own advantage. It is excellent, we must all allow. Yet this government never of itself furthered any enterprise, but by the alacrity with which it got out of its way.

It does not keep the country free. *It* does not settle the West. *It* does not educate. The character inherent in the American people has done all that has been accomplished; and it would have done somewhat more, if the government had not sometimes got in its way. For government is an expedient by which men would fain succeed in letting one another alone; and, as has been said, when it is most expedient, the governed are most let alone by it. Trade and commerce, if they were not made of India rubber, would never manage to bounce over the obstacles which legislators are continually putting in their way; and, if one were to judge these men wholly by the effects of their actions, and not partly by their intentions, they would deserve to be classed and punished with those mischievous persons who put obstructions on the railroads.

But, to speak practically and as a citizen, unlike those who call themselves no-government men, I ask for, not at once no government, but *at once* a better government. Let every man make known what kind of government would command his respect, and that will be one step toward obtaining it.

After all, the practical reason why, when the power is once in the hands of the people, a majority are permitted, and for a long period continue, to rule, is not because they are most likely to be in the right, nor because this seems fairest to the minority, but because they are physically the strongest. But a government in which the majority rule in all cases cannot be based on justice, even as far as men understand it. Can there not be a government in which majorities do not virtually decide right and wrong, but conscience?—in which majorities decide only those questions to which the rule of expediency is applicable? Must the citizen ever for a moment, or in the least degree, resign his conscience to the legislator? Why has every man a conscience, then? I think that we should be men first, and subjects afterward. It is not desirable to cultivate a respect for the law, so much as for the right. The only obligation which I have a right to assume is to do at any time what I think right. It is truly enough said that a corporation has no conscience; but a corporation of conscientious men is a corporation *with* a conscience. Law never made men a whit more just; and, by means of their respect for it, even the well-disposed are daily made the agents of injustice. . . .

How does it become a man to behave toward this American government today? I answer, that he cannot without disgrace be associated with it. I cannot for an instant recognize that political organization as *my* government which is the *slave's* government also.

All men recognize the right of revolution; that is, the right to refuse allegiance to, and to resist, the government, when its tyranny or its inefficiency are great and unendurable. But almost all say that such is not the case now. But such was the case, they think, in the Revolution of '75. If one were to tell me that this was a bad government because it taxed certain foreign commodities brought to its ports, it is most probable that I should not make an ado about it, for I can do without them. All machines have their friction; and possibly this does enough good to counterbalance the evil. At any rate, it is a great evil to make a stir about it. But when the friction comes to have its machine, and oppression and robbery are organized, I say, let us not have such a machine any longer. In other words, when a sixth of the population of a nation which has undertaken to be the refuge of liberty are slaves, and a whole country is unjustly overrun and conquered by a foreign army, and subjected to military law, I think that it is not too soon for honest men to rebel and revolutionize. What makes this duty the more urgent is the fact that the country so overrun is not our own, but ours is the invading army. . . .

There are thousands who are *in opinion* opposed to slavery and to the war, who yet in effect do nothing to put an end to them; who, esteeming themselves children of Washington and Franklin, sit down with their hands in their pockets, and say that they know not what to do, and do nothing; who even postpone the question of freedom to the question of free-trade, and quietly read the prices-current along with the latest advices from Mexico, after dinner, and, it may be, fall asleep over them both. What is the price-current of an honest man and patriot today? They hesitate, and they regret, and sometimes they petition; but they do nothing in earnest and with effect. They will wait, well disposed, for others to remedy the evil, that they may no longer have it to regret. At most, they give only a cheap vote, and a feeble countenance and Godspeed, to the right, as it goes by them. There are nine hundred and ninety-nine patrons of virtue to one virtuous man; but it is easier to deal with the real possessor of a thing than with the temporary guardian of it. . . .

There is but little virtue in the action of masses of men. When the majority shall at length vote for the abolition of slavery, it will be because they are indifferent to slavery, or because there is but little slavery left to be abolished by their vote. *They* will then be the only slaves. Only *his* vote can hasten the abolition of slavery who asserts his own freedom by his vote. . . .

It is not a man's duty, as a matter of course, to devote himself to the eradication of any, even the most enormous wrong; he may still properly have other concerns to engage him; but it is his duty, at least, to wash his hands of it, and, if he gives it no thought longer, not to give it practically his support. If I devote myself to other pursuits and contemplations, I must first see, at least, that I do not pursue them sitting upon another man's shoulders. I must get off him first, that he may pursue his contemplations too. See what gross inconsistency is tolerated. I have heard some of my townsmen say, "I should like to have them order me out to help put down an insurrection of the slaves, or to march to Mexico;—see if I would go"; and yet these very men have each, directly by their allegiance, and so indirectly, at least, by their money, furnished a substitute. The soldier is applauded who refuses to serve in an unjust war by those who do not refuse to sustain the unjust government which makes the war; is applauded by those whose own act and authority he disregards and sets at naught; as if the state were penitent to that degree that it hired one to scourge it while it sinned, but not to that degree that it left off sinning for a moment. Thus, under the name of Order and Civil Government, we are all made at last to pay homage to and support our own meanness. After the first blush of sin comes its indifference;

and from immoral it becomes, as it were, *un*moral, and not quite unnecessary to that life which we have made.

The broadest and most prevalent error requires the most disinterested virtue to sustain it. The slight reproach to which the virtue of patriotism is commonly liable, the noble are most likely to incur. Those who, while they disapprove of the character and measures of a government, yield to it their allegiance and support are undoubtedly its most conscientious supporters, and so frequently the most serious obstacles to reform. Some are petitioning the State to dissolve the Union, to disregard the requisitions of the President. Why do they not dissolve it themselves—the union between themselves and the State—and refuse to pay their quota into its treasury? Do not they stand in the same relation to the State that the State does to the Union? And have not the same reasons prevented the State from resisting the Union which have prevented them from resisting the State?

How can a man be satisfied to entertain an opinion merely, and enjoy *it?* Is there any enjoyment in it, if his opinion is that he is aggrieved? If you are cheated out of a single dollar by your neighbor, you do not rest satisfied with knowing that you are cheated, or with saying that you are cheated, or even with petitioning him to pay you your due; but you take effectual steps at once to obtain the full amount, and see that you are never cheated again. Action from principle, the perception and the performance of right, changes things and relations; it is essentially revolutionary, and does not consist wholly with anything which was. It not only divides states and churches, it divides families; ay, it divides the *individual*, separating the diabolical in him from the divine.

Unjust laws exist; shall we be content to obey them, or shall we endeavor to amend them, and obey them until we have succeeded, or shall we transgress them at once? Men generally, under such a government as this, think that they ought to wait until they have persuaded the majority to alter them. They think that, if they should resist, the remedy would be worse than the evil. But it is the fault of the government itself that the remedy *is* worse than the evil. *It* makes it worse. Why is it not more apt to anticipate and provide for reform? Why does it not cherish its wise minority? Why does it cry and resist before it is hurt? Why does it not encourage its citizens to be on the alert to point out its faults, and *do* better than it would have them? Why does it always crucify Christ, and excommunicate Copernicus and Luther, and pronounce Washington and Franklin rebels? . . .

If the injustice is part of the necessary friction of the machine of government, let it go, let it go; perchance it will wear smooth—certainly the machine will wear out. If the injustice has a spring, or a pulley, or a rope, or a crank, exclusively for itself, then perhaps you may consider whether the remedy will not be worse than the evil; but if it is of such a nature that it requires you to be the agent of injustice to another, then, I say, break the law. Let your life be a counter friction to stop the machine. What I have to do is to see, at any rate, that I do not lend myself to the wrong which I condemn.

As for adopting the ways which the State has provided for remedying the evil, I know not of such ways. They take too much time, and a man's life will be gone. I have other affairs to attend to. I came into this world, not chiefly to make this a good place to live in, but to live in it, be it good or bad. A man has not everything to do, but something; and because he cannot do *everything*, it is not necessary that he should do *something* wrong. It is not my business to be petitioning the Governor or the Legislature any more than it is theirs to petition me; and if they should not hear my petition, what should I do then? But in this case the State has provided no way; its very Constitution is the evil. This may seem to be harsh and stubborn and unconciliatory; but it is to treat with the utmost kindness and consideration the only spirit that can appreciate or deserves it. So is all change for the better, like birth and death which convulse the body.

I do not hesitate to say, that those who call themselves Abolitionists should at once effectually withdraw their support, both in person and property, from the government of Massachusetts, and not wait till they constitute a majority of one, before they suffer the right to prevail through them. I think that it is enough if they have God on their side, without waiting for that other one. Moreover, any man more right than his neighbors constitutes a majority of one already. . . .

I know this well, that if one thousand, if one hundred, if ten men whom I could name—if ten *honest* men only—ay, if *one* HONEST man, in this State of Massachusetts, *ceasing to hold slaves*, were actually to withdraw from this copartnership, and be locked up in the county jail therefor, it would be the abolition of slavery in America. For it matters not how small the beginning may seem to be: what is once well done is done forever. But we love better to talk about it: that we say is our mission. Reform keeps many scores of newspapers in its service, but not one man. If my esteemed neighbor, the State's ambassador, who will devote his days to the settlement of the question of human rights in the Council Chamber, instead of being threatened with the prisons of Carolina, were to sit down the prisoner of Massachusetts, that State which is so anxious to foist the sin of slavery upon her sister—though at present she can discover only an act of inhospitality to be the ground of a quarrel with her—the Legislature would not wholly waive the subject the following winter.

Under a government which imprisons any unjustly, the true place for a just man is also a prison. The proper place today, the only place which Massachusetts has provided for her freer and less desponding spirits, is in her prisons, to be put out and locked out of the State by her own act, as they have already put themselves out by their principles. It is there that the fugitive slave, and the Mexican prisoner on parole, and the Indian come to plead the wrongs of his race, should find them; on that separate, but more free and honorable ground, where the State places those who are not *with* her, but *against* her—the only house in a slave State in which a free man can abide with honor. If any think that their influence would be lost there, and their voices no longer afflict the ear of the State, that they would not be as an enemy within its walls, they do not know by how much truth is stronger than error, nor how much more eloquently and effectively he can combat injustice who has experienced a little in his own person. Cast your whole vote, not a strip of paper merely, but your whole influence. A minority is powerless while it conforms to the majority; it is not even a minority then; but it is irresistible when it clogs by its whole weight. If the alternative is to keep all just men in prison, or give up war and slavery, the State will not hesitate which to choose. If a thousand men were not to pay their tax-bills this year, that would not be a violent and bloody measure, as it would be to pay them, and enable the State to commit violence and shed innocent blood. This is, in fact, the definition of a peaceable revolution, if any such is possible. If the tax-gatherer, or any other public officer, asks me, as one has done, "But what shall I do?" my answer is, "If you really wish to do anything, resign your office." When the subject has refused allegiance, and the officer has resigned his office, then the revolution is accomplished. But even suppose blood should flow. Is there not a sort of blood shed when the conscience is wounded? Through this wound a man's real manhood and immortality flow out, and he bleeds to an everlasting death. I see this blood flowing now. . . .

Some years ago, the State met me in behalf of the Church, and commanded me to pay a certain sum toward the support of a clergyman whose preaching my father attended, but never I myself. "Pay," it said, "or be locked up in the jail." I declined to pay. But, unfortunately, another man saw fit to pay it. I did not see why the schoolmaster should be taxed to support the priest, and not the priest the schoolmaster: for I was not the State's schoolmaster, but I supported myself by voluntary subscription. I did not see why the lyceum should not present its tax-bill, and have the State to back its demand, as well as the Church. However, at the request of the selectmen, I condescended to make some such statement as this in writing:—"Know all men by these presents, that I, Henry Thoreau, do not wish to be regarded as a member of any incorporated society which I have not joined." This I gave to the town clerk; and he has it. The State, having thus learned that I did not wish to be regarded as a member of that church, has never made a like demand on me since; though it said that it must adhere to its original presumption that time. If I had known how to name them, I should then have signed off in detail from all the societies which I never signed on to; but I did not know where to find a complete list.

I have paid no poll tax for six years. I was put into a jail once on this account, for one night; and, as I stood considering the walls of solid stone, two or three feet thick, the door of wood and iron, a foot thick, and the iron grating which strained the light, I could not help being struck with the foolishness of that institution which treated me as if I were mere flesh and blood and bones, to be locked up. I wondered that it should have concluded at length that this was the best use it could put me to, and had never thought to avail itself of my services in some way. I saw that, if there was a wall of stone between me and my townsmen, there was a still more difficult one to climb or break through, before they could get to be as free as I was. I did not for a moment feel confined, and the walls seemed a great waste of stone and mortar. I felt as if I alone of all my townsmen had paid my tax. They plainly did not know how to treat me, but behaved like persons who are underbred. In every threat and in every compliment there was a blunder; for they thought that my chief desire was to stand the other side of that stone wall. I could not but smile to see how industriously they locked the door on my meditations, which followed them out again without let or hindrance, and *they* were really all that was dangerous. As they could not reach me, they had resolved to punish my body; just as boys, if they cannot come at some person against whom they have a spite, will abuse his dog. I saw that the State was half-witted, that it was timid as a lone woman with her silver spoons, and that it did not know its friends from its foes, and I lost all my remaining respect for it, and pitied it. . . .

It was formerly the custom in our village, when a poor debtor came out of jail, for his acquaintances to salute him, looking through their fingers, which were crossed to represent the grating of a jail window, "How do ye do?" My neighbors did not thus salute me, but first looked at me, and then at one another, as if

I had returned from a long journey. I was put into jail as I was going to the shoemaker's to get a shoe which was mended. When I was let out the next morning, I proceeded to finish my errand, and, having put on my mended shoe, joined a huckleberry party, who were impatient to put themselves under my conduct; and in half an hour—for the horse was soon tackled—was in the midst of a huckleberry field, on one of our highest hills, two miles off, and then the State was nowhere to be seen. . . .

I believe that the State will soon be able to take all my work of this sort out of my hands, and then I shall be no better a patriot than my fellow-countrymen. Seen from a lower point of view, the Constitution, with all its faults, is very good; the law and the courts are very respectable; even this State and this American government are, in many respects, very admirable and rare things, to be thankful for, such as a great many have described them; but seen from a point of view a little higher, they are what I have described them; seen from a higher still, and the highest, who shall say what they are, or that they are worth looking at or thinking of at all?

However, the government does not concern me much, and I shall bestow the fewest possible thoughts on it. It is not many moments that I live under a government, even in this world. If a man is thought-free, fancy-free, imagination-free, that which *is not* never for a long time appearing *to be* to him, unwise rulers or reformers cannot fatally interrupt him. . . .

They who know of no purer sources of truth, who have traced up its stream no higher, stand, and wisely stand, by the Bible and the Constitution, and drink at it there with reverence and humility; but they who behold where it comes trickling into this lake or that pool, gird up their loins once more, and continue their pilgrimage toward its fountain-head.

No man with a genius for legislation has appeared in America. They are rare in the history of the world. There are orators, politicians, and eloquent men, by the thousand; but the speaker has not yet opened his mouth to speak who is capable of settling the much-vexed questions of the day. We love eloquence for its own sake, and not for any truth which it may utter, or any heroism it may inspire. Our legislators have not yet learned the comparative value of free-trade and of freedom, of union, and of rectitude, to a nation. They have no genius or talent for comparatively humble questions of taxation and finance, commerce and manufactures and agriculture. If we were left solely to the wordy wit of legislators in Congress for our guidance, uncorrected by the seasonable experience and the effectual complaints of the people, America would not long retain her rank among the nations. For eighteen hundred years, though perchance I have no right to say it, the New Testament has been written; yet where is the legislator who has wisdom and practical talent enough to avail himself of the light which it sheds on the science of legislation?

The authority of government, even such as I am willing to submit to—for I will cheerfully obey those who know and can do better than I, and in many things even those who neither know nor can do so well—is still an impure one: to be strictly just, it must have the sanction and consent of the governed. It can have no pure right over my person and property but what I concede to it. The progress from an absolute to a limited monarchy, from a limited monarchy to a democracy, is a progress toward a true respect for the individual. Even the Chinese philosopher was wise enough to regard the individual as the basis of the empire. Is a democracy, such as we know it, the last improvement possible in government? Is it not possible to take a step further towards recognizing and organizing the rights of man? There will never be a really free and enlightened State until the State comes to recognize the individual as a higher and independent power, from which all its own power and authority are derived, and treats him accordingly. I please myself with imagining a State at least which can afford to be just to all men, and to treat the individual with respect as a neighbor; which even would not think it inconsistent with its own repose if a few were to live aloof from it, not meddling with it, nor embraced by it, who fulfilled all the duties of neighbors and fellow-men. A State which bore this kind of fruit, and suffered it to drop off as fast as it ripened, would prepare the way for a still more perfect and glorious State, which also I have imagined, but not yet anywhere seen.

WALKING

"Walking" began as a lecture delivered at the Concord Lyceum on April 23, 1851, and was repeated on ten different occasions after that. Thoreau saw the essay, regarded today as a seminal work for the modern environmental movement, as foundational to his thinking. "I regard it as a sort of introduction to all that I may write hereafter," he wrote of the essay, which was first published posthumously in the Atlantic Monthly *a month after his death in 1862.*

I wish to speak a word for Nature, for absolute freedom and wildness, as contrasted with a freedom and culture merely civil—to regard man as an inhabitant, or a part and parcel of Nature, rather than a member of society. I wish to make an extreme statement, if so I may make an emphatic one, for there are enough champions of civilization: the minister and the school committee and every one of you will take care of that.

I have met with but one or two persons in the course of my life who understood the art of Walking, that is, of taking walks—who had a genius, so to speak, for *sauntering*, which word is beautifully derived "from idle people who roved about the country, in the Middle Ages, and asked charity, under pretense of going *à la Sainte Terre*," to the Holy Land, till the children exclaimed, "There goes a *Sainte-Terrer*," a Saunterer, a Holy-Lander. They who never go to the Holy Land in their walks, as they pretend, are indeed mere idlers and vagabonds; but they who do go there are saunterers in the good sense, such as I mean. Some, however, would derive the word from *sans terre* without land or a home, which, therefore, in the good sense, will mean, having no particular home, but equally at home everywhere. For this is the secret of successful sauntering. He who sits still in a house all the time may be the greatest vagrant of all; but the saunterer, in the good sense, is no more vagrant than the meandering river, which is all the while sedulously seeking the shortest course to the sea. But I prefer the first, which, indeed, is the most probable derivation. For every walk is a sort of crusade, preached by some Peter the Hermit in us, to go forth and reconquer this Holy Land from the hands of the Infidels.

It is true, we are but faint-hearted crusaders, even the walkers, nowadays, who undertake no persevering, never-ending enterprises. Our expeditions are but tours, and come round again at evening to the old hearth-side from which we set out. Half the walk is but retracing our steps. We should go forth on the shortest walk, perchance, in the spirit of undying adventure, never to return—prepared to send back our embalmed hearts only as relics to our desolate kingdoms. If you are ready to leave father and mother, and brother and sister, and wife and child and friends, and never see them again—if you have paid your debts, and made your will, and settled all your affairs, and are a free man—then you are ready for a walk.

To come down to my own experience, my companion and I, for I sometimes have a companion, take pleasure in fancying ourselves knights of a new, or rather an old, order—not Equestrians or Chevaliers, not Ritters or Riders, but Walkers, a still more ancient and honorable class, I trust. The chivalric and heroic spirit which once belonged to the Rider seems now to reside in, or perchance to have subsided into, the Walker—not the Knight, but Walker, Errant. He is a sort of fourth estate, outside of Church and State and People.

We have felt that we almost alone hereabouts practiced this noble art; though, to tell the truth, at least if their own assertions are to be received, most of my townsmen would fain walk sometimes, as I do, but they cannot. No wealth can buy the requisite leisure, freedom, and independence which are the capital in this profession. It comes only by the grace of God. It requires a direct dispensation from Heaven to become a walker. You must be born into the family of the Walkers. *Ambulator nascitur, non fit*. Some of my townsmen, it is true, can remember and have described to me some walks which they took ten years ago, in which they were so blessed as to lose themselves for half an hour in the woods; but I know very well that they have confined themselves to the highway ever since, whatever pretensions they may make to belong to this select class. No doubt they were elevated for a moment as by the reminiscence of a previous state of existence, when even they were foresters and outlaws. . . .

I think that I cannot preserve my health and spirits, unless I spend four hours a day at least—and it is commonly more than that—sauntering through the woods and over the hills and fields, absolutely free from all worldly engagements. You may safely say, A penny for your thoughts, or a thousand pounds. When sometimes I am reminded that the mechanics and shopkeepers stay in their shops not only all the forenoon, but all the afternoon too, sitting with crossed legs, so many of them—as if the legs were made to sit upon, and not to stand or walk upon—I think that they deserve some credit for not having all committed suicide long ago.

I, who cannot stay in my chamber for a single day without acquiring some rust, and when sometimes I have stolen forth for a walk at the eleventh hour, or four o'clock in the afternoon, too late to redeem the day, when the shades of night were already beginning to be mingled with the daylight, have felt as if I had committed some sin to be atoned for,—I confess that I am astonished at the power of endurance, to say nothing of the moral insensibility, of my neighbors who confine themselves to shops and offices the whole day for weeks and months, aye, and years almost together. I know not what manner of stuff they are of—sitting there now at three o'clock in the afternoon, as if it were three o'clock in the morning. Bonaparte may talk of the three-o'clock-in-the-morning courage, but it is nothing to the courage which can sit down cheerfully at this hour in the afternoon over against one's self whom you have known all the morning, to starve out a garrison to whom you are bound by such strong ties of sympathy. I wonder that about this time, or say between four and five o'clock in the afternoon, too late for the morning papers and too early for the evening ones, there is not a general explosion heard up and down the street, scattering a legion of antiquated and house-bred notions and whims to the four winds for an airing—and so the evil cure itself.

How womankind, who are confined to the house still more than men, stand it I do not know; but I have ground to suspect that most of them do not *stand* it at all. When, early in a summer afternoon, we have been shaking the dust of the village from the skirts of our garments, making haste past those houses with purely Doric or Gothic fronts, which have such an air of repose about them, my companion whispers that probably about these times their occupants are all gone to bed. Then it is that I appreciate the beauty and the glory of architecture, which itself never turns in, but forever stands out and erect, keeping watch over the slumberers.

No doubt temperament, and, above all, age, have a good deal to do with it. As a man grows older, his ability to sit still and follow indoor occupations increases. He grows vespertinal in his habits as the evening of life approaches, till at last he comes forth only just before sundown, and gets all the walk that he requires in half an hour.

But the walking of which I speak has nothing in it akin to taking exercise, as it is called, as the sick take medicine at stated hours—as the swinging of dumbbells or chairs; but is itself the enterprise and adventure of the day. If you would get exercise, go in search of the springs of life. Think of a man's swinging dumbbells for his health, when those springs are bubbling up in far-off pastures unsought by him!

Moreover, you must walk like a camel, which is said to be the only beast which ruminates when walking. When a traveler asked Wordsworth's servant to show him her master's study, she answered, "Here is his library, but his study is out of doors."

Living much out of doors, in the sun and wind, will no doubt produce a certain roughness of character—will cause a thicker cuticle to grow over some of the finer qualities of our nature, as on the face and hands, or as severe manual labor robs the hands of some of their delicacy of touch. So staying in the house, on the other hand, may produce a softness and smoothness, not to say thinness of skin, accompanied by an increased sensibility to certain impressions. Perhaps we should be more susceptible to some influences important to our intellectual and moral growth, if the sun had shone and the wind blown on us a little less; and no doubt it is a nice matter to proportion rightly the thick and thin skin. But methinks that is a scurf that will fall off fast enough—that the natural remedy is to be found in the proportion which the night bears to the day, the winter to the summer, thought to experience. There will be so much the more air and sunshine in our thoughts. The callous palms of the laborer are conversant with finer tissues of self-respect and heroism, whose touch thrills the heart, than the languid fingers of idleness. That is mere sentimentality that lies abed by day and thinks itself white, far from the tan and callus of experience. . . .

Life consists with wildness. The most alive is the wildest. Not yet subdued to man, its presence refreshes him. One who pressed forward incessantly and never rested from his labors, who grew fast and made infinite demands on life, would always find himself in a new country or wilderness, and surrounded by the raw material of life. He would be climbing over the prostrate stems of primitive forest-trees.

Hope and the future for me are not in lawns and cultivated fields, not in towns and cities, but in the impervious and quaking swamps. When, formerly, I have analyzed my partiality for some farm which I had contemplated purchasing, I have frequently found that I was attracted solely by a few square rods of impermeable and unfathomable bog—a natural sink in one corner of it. That was the jewel which dazzled me. I derive more of my subsistence from the swamps which surround my native town than from the cultivated gardens in the village. There are no richer parterres to my eyes than the dense beds of dwarf andromeda (*Cassandra calyculata*) which cover these tender places on the earth's surface. Botany cannot go farther than tell me the names of the shrubs which grow there—the high blueberry, panicled andromeda, lambkill, azalea, and rhodora—all standing in the quaking sphagnum. I often think that I should like to have my house front on this mass of dull red bushes, omitting other flower plots and borders, transplanted spruce and trim box, even graveled walks—to have this fertile spot under my windows, not a few imported barrowfuls of soil only to cover the sand which was thrown out in digging the cellar. Why not put my house, my parlor, behind this plot, instead of behind that meager assemblage of curiosities, that poor apology for a Nature and Art, which I call my front yard? It is an effort to clear up and make a decent appearance when the carpenter and mason have departed, though done as much for the passer-by as the dweller within. The most tasteful front-yard fence was never an agreeable object of study to me; the most elaborate ornaments, acorn tops, or what not, soon wearied and disgusted me. Bring your sills up to the very edge of the swamp, then (though it may not be the best place for a dry cellar), so that there be no access on that side to citizens. Front yards are not made to walk in, but, at most, through, and you could go in the back way.

Yes, though you may think me perverse, if it were proposed to me to dwell in the neighborhood of the most beautiful garden that ever human art contrived, or else of a Dismal Swamp, I should certainly decide for the swamp. How vain, then, have been all your labors, citizens, for me!

My spirits infallibly rise in proportion to the outward dreariness. Give me the ocean, the desert, or the wilderness! In the desert, pure air and solitude compensate for want of moisture and fertility. . . . When I would recreate myself, I seek the darkest wood, the thickest and most interminable and, to the citizen, most dismal, swamp. I enter a swamp as a sacred place,—a *sanctum sanctorum*. There is the strength, the marrow, of Nature. The wildwood covers the virgin mould,—and the same soil is good for men and for trees. A man's health requires as many acres of meadow to his prospect as his farm does loads of muck. There are the strong meats on which he feeds. A town is saved, not more by the righteous men in it than by the woods and swamps that surround it. A township where one primitive forest waves above while another primitive forest rots below—such a town is fitted to raise not only corn and potatoes, but poets and philosophers for the coming ages. In such a soil grew Homer and Confucius and the rest, and out of such a wilderness comes the Reformer eating locusts and wild honey.

To preserve wild animals implies generally the creation of a forest for them to dwell in or resort to. So it is with man. . . .

The civilized nations—Greece, Rome, England—have been sustained by the primitive forests which anciently rotted where they stand. They survive as long as the soil is not exhausted. Alas for human culture! little is to be expected of a nation, when the vegetable mould is exhausted, and it is compelled to make manure of the bones of its fathers. There the poet sustains himself merely by his own superfluous fat, and the philosopher comes down on his marrow-bones.

It is said to be the task of the American "to work the virgin soil," and that "agriculture here already assumes proportions unknown everywhere else." I think that the farmer displaces the Indian even because he redeems the meadow, and so makes himself stronger and in some respects more natural. I was surveying for a man the other day a single straight line one hundred and thirty-two rods long, through a swamp at whose entrance might have been written the words which Dante read over the entrance to the infernal regions,—"Leave all hope, ye that enter"—that is, of ever getting out again; where at one time I saw my employer actually up to his neck and swimming for his life in his property, though it was still winter. He had another similar swamp which I could not survey at all, because it was completely under water, and nevertheless, with regard to a third swamp, which I did *survey* from a distance, he remarked to me, true to his instincts, that he would not part with it for any consideration, on account of the mud which it contained. And that man intends to put a girdling ditch round the whole in the course of forty months, and so redeem it by the magic of his spade. I refer to him only as the type of a class.

The weapons with which we have gained our most important victories, which should be handed down as heirlooms from father to son, are not the sword and the lance, but the bushwhack, the turf-cutter, the spade, and the bog hoe, rusted with the blood of many a meadow, and begrimed with the dust of many a hard-fought field. The very winds blew the Indian's cornfield into the meadow, and pointed out the way which he had not the skill to follow. He had no better implement with which to intrench himself in the land than a clamshell. But the farmer is armed with plow and spade.

In literature it is only the wild that attracts us. Dullness is but another name for tameness. It is the uncivilized free and wild thinking in Hamlet and the Iliad, in all the scriptures and mythologies, not learned in the schools, that delights us. As the wild duck is more swift and beautiful than the tame, so is the wild—the mallard—thought, which 'mid falling dews wings its way above the fens. A truly good book is something as natural, and as unexpectedly and unaccountably fair and perfect, as a wildflower discovered on the prairies of the West or in the jungles of the East. Genius is a light which makes the darkness visible, like the lightning's flash, which perchance shatters the temple of knowledge itself—and not a taper lighted at the hearthstone of the race, which pales before the light of common day.

English literature, from the days of the minstrels to the Lake Poets—Chaucer and Spenser and Milton, and even Shakespeare, included—breathes no quite fresh and, in this sense, wild strain. It is an essentially tame and civilized literature, reflecting Greece and Rome. Her wilderness is a greenwood, her wild man a Robin Hood. There is plenty of genial love of Nature, but not so much of Nature herself. Her chronicles inform us when her wild animals, but not when the wild man in her, became extinct.

The science of Humboldt is one thing, poetry is another thing. The poet today, notwithstanding all the discoveries of science, and the accumulated learning of mankind, enjoys no advantage over Homer.

Where is the literature which gives expression to Nature? He would be a poet who could impress the winds and streams into his service, to speak for him; who nailed words to their primitive senses, as farmers drive down stakes in the spring, which the frost has heaved; who derived his words as often as he used them, transplanted them to his page with earth adhering to their roots; whose words were so true and fresh and natural that they would appear to expand like the buds at the approach of spring, though they lay half smothered between two musty leaves in a library—aye, to bloom and bear fruit there, after their kind, annually, for the faithful reader, in sympathy with surrounding Nature. . . .

In short, all good things are wild and free. There is something in a strain of music, whether produced by an instrument or by the human voice—take the sound of a bugle in a summer night, for instance—which by its wildness, to speak without satire, reminds me of the cries emitted by wild beasts in their native forests. It is so much of their wildness as I can understand. Give me for my friends and neighbors wild men, not tame ones. The wildness of the savage is but a faint symbol of the awful ferity with which good men and lovers meet.

I love even to see the domestic animals reassert their native rights—any evidence that they have not wholly lost their original wild habits and vigor; as when my neighbor's cow breaks out of her pasture early in the spring and boldly swims the river, a cold, gray tide, twenty-five or thirty rods wide, swollen by the melted snow. It is the buffalo crossing the Mississippi. This exploit confers some dignity on the herd in my eyes, already dignified. The seeds of instinct are preserved under the thick hides of cattle and horses, like seeds in the bowels of the earth, an indefinite period. . . .

I rejoice that horses and steers have to be broken before they can be made the slaves of men, and that men themselves have some wild oats still left to sow before they become submissive members of society. Undoubtedly, all men are not equally fit subjects for civilization; and because the majority, like dogs and sheep, are tame by inherited disposition, this is no reason why the others should have their natures broken that they may be reduced to the same level. Men are in the main alike, but they were made several in order that they might be various. If a low use is to be served, one man will do nearly or quite as well as another; if a high one, individual excellence is to be regarded. . . .

Here is this vast, savage, howling mother of ours, Nature, lying all around, with such beauty, and such affection for her children, as the leopard; and yet we are so early weaned from her breast to society, to that culture which is exclusively an interaction of man on man—a sort of breeding in and in, which produces at most a merely English nobility, a civilization destined to have a speedy limit.

In society, in the best institutions of men, it is easy to detect a certain precocity. When we should still be growing children, we are already little men. Give me a culture which imports much muck from the meadows, and deepens the soil—not that which trusts to heating manures, and improved implements and modes of culture only! . . .

I would not have every man nor every part of a man cultivated, any more than I would have every acre of earth cultivated: part will be tillage, but the greater part will be meadow and forest, not only serving an immediate use, but preparing a mould against a distant future, by the annual decay of the vegetation which it supports. . . .

We have heard of a Society for the Diffusion of Useful Knowledge. It is said that knowledge is power, and the like. Methinks there is equal need of a Society for the Diffusion of Useful Ignorance, what we will call Beautiful Knowledge, a knowledge useful in a higher sense: for what is most of our boasted so-called knowledge but a conceit that we know something, which robs us of the advantage of our actual ignorance? What we call knowledge is often our positive ignorance; ignorance our negative knowledge. By long years of patient industry and reading of the newspapers—for what are the libraries of science but files of newspapers?—a man accumulates a myriad facts, lays them up in his memory, and then when in some spring of his life he saunters abroad into the Great Fields of thought, he, as it were, goes to grass like a horse and leaves all his harness behind in the stable. I would say to the Society for the Diffusion of Useful Knowledge, sometimes,—Go to grass. You have eaten hay long enough. The spring has come with its green crop. The very cows are driven to their country pastures before the end of May; though I have heard of one unnatural farmer who kept his cow in the barn and fed her on hay all the year round. So, frequently, the Society for the Diffusion of Useful Knowledge treats its cattle. . . .

Live free, child of the mist—and with respect to knowledge we are all children of the mist. The man who takes the liberty to live is superior to all the laws, by virtue of his relation to the lawmaker. "That is active duty," says the Vishnu Purana, "which is not for our bondage; that is knowledge which is for our liberation: all other duty is good only unto weariness; all other knowledge is only the cleverness of an artist. . . ."

While almost all men feel an attraction drawing them to society, few are attracted strongly to Nature. In their reaction to Nature men appear to me for the most part, notwithstanding their arts, lower than the animals. It is not often a beautiful relation, as in the case of the animals. How little appreciation of the beauty of the land-scape there is among us! We have to be told that the Greeks called the world Kósmos, Beauty, or Order, but we do not see clearly why they did so, and we esteem it at best only a curious philological fact.

For my part, I feel that with regard to Nature I live a sort of border life, on the confines of a world into which I make occasional and transient forays only, and my patriotism and allegiance to the state into whose territories I seem to retreat are those of a moss-trooper. Unto a life which I call natural I would gladly follow even a will-o'-the-wisp through bogs and sloughs unimaginable, but no moon nor firefly has shown me the causeway to it. Nature is a personality so vast and universal that we have never seen one of her features. The walker in the familiar fields which stretch around my native town sometimes finds himself in another land than is described in their owners' deeds, as it were in some faraway field on the confines of the actual Concord, where her jurisdiction ceases, and the idea which the word Concord suggests ceases to be suggested. These farms which I have myself surveyed, these bounds which I have set up, appear dimly still as through a mist; but they have no chemistry to fix them; they fade from the surface of the glass, and the picture which the painter painted stands out dimly from beneath. The world with which we are commonly acquainted leaves no trace, and it will have no anniversary.

I took a walk on Spaulding's Farm the other afternoon. I saw the setting sun lighting up the opposite side of a stately pine wood. Its golden rays straggled into the aisles of the wood as into some noble hall. I was impressed as if some ancient and altogether admirable and shining family had settled there in that part of the land called Concord, unknown to me, to whom the sun was servant, who had not gone into society in the village, who had not been called on. I saw their park, their pleasure-ground, beyond through the wood, in Spaulding's cranberry-meadow. The pines furnished them with gables as they grew. Their house was not obvious to vision; the trees grew through it. I do not know whether I heard the sounds of a suppressed hilarity or not. They seemed to recline on the sunbeams. They have sons and daughters. They are quite well. The farmer's cart-path, which leads directly through their hall, does not in the least put them out, as the muddy bottom of a pool is sometimes seen through the reflected skies. They never heard of Spaulding, and do not know that he is their neighbor, notwithstanding I heard him whistle as he drove his team through the house. Nothing can equal the serenity of their lives. Their coat-of-arms is simply a lichen. I saw it painted on the pines and oaks. Their attics were in the tops of the trees. They are of no politics. There was no noise of labor. I did not perceive that they were weaving or spinning. Yet I did detect, when the wind lulled and hearing was done away, the finest imaginable sweet musical hum,—as of a distant hive in May,— which perchance was the sound of their thinking. They had no idle thoughts, and no one without could see their work, for their industry was not as in knots and excrescences embayed. . . .

Above all, we cannot afford not to live in the present. He is blessed over all mortals who loses no moment of the passing life in remembering the past. Unless our philosophy hears the cock crow in every barnyard within our horizon, it is belated. That sound commonly reminds us that we are growing rusty and antique in our employments and habits of thoughts. His philosophy comes down to a more recent time than ours. There is something suggested by it that is a newer testament,—the gospel according to this moment. He has not fallen astern; he has got up early and kept up early, and to be where he is is to be in season, in the foremost rank of time. It is an expression of the health and soundness of Nature, a brag for all the world,—healthiness as of a spring burst forth, a new fountain of the Muses, to celebrate this last instant of time. Where he lives no fugitive slave laws are passed. Who has not betrayed his master many times since last he heard that note?

The merit of this bird's strain is in its freedom from all plaintiveness. The singer can easily move us to tears or to laughter, but where is he who can excite in us a pure morning joy? When, in doleful dumps, breaking the awful stillness of our wooden sidewalk on a Sunday, or, perchance, a watcher in the house of mourning, I hear a cockerel crow far or near, I think to myself, "There is one of us well, at any rate,"—and with a sudden gush return to my senses.

We had a remarkable sunset one day last November. I was walking in a meadow, the source of a small brook, when the sun at last, just before setting, after a cold, gray day, reached a clear stratum in the horizon, and the softest, brightest morning sunlight fell on the dry grass and on the stems of the trees in the opposite horizon and on the leaves of the shrub oaks on the hillside, while our shadows stretched long over the meadow eastward, as if we were the only motes in its beams. It was such a light as we could not have imagined a moment before, and the air also was so warm and serene that nothing was wanting to make a paradise of that meadow. When we reflected that this was not a solitary phenomenon, never to happen again, but that it would happen forever and ever, an infinite number of evenings, and cheer and reassure the latest child that walked there, it was more glorious still.

The sun sets on some retired meadow, where no house is visible, with all the glory and splendor that it lavishes on cities, and perchance as it has never set before—where there is but a solitary marsh hawk to have his wings gilded by it, or only a musquash looks out from his cabin, and there is some little black-veined brook in the midst of the marsh, just beginning to meander, winding slowly round a decaying stump. We walked in so pure and bright a light, gilding the withered grass and leaves, so softly and serenely bright, I thought I had never bathed in such a golden flood, without a ripple or a murmur to it. The west side of every wood and rising ground gleamed like the boundary of Elysium, and the sun on our backs seemed like a gentle herdsman driving us home at evening.

So we saunter toward the Holy Land, till one day the sun shall shine more brightly than ever he has done, shall perchance shine into our minds and hearts, and light up our whole lives with a great awakening light, as warm and serene and golden as on a bank side in autumn.

7

Walden

SOLITUDE

This is a delicious evening, when the whole body is one sense, and imbibes delight through every pore. I go and come with a strange liberty in Nature, a part of herself. As I walk along the stony shore of the pond in my shirt-sleeves, though it is cool as well as cloudy and windy, and I see nothing special to attract me, all the elements are unusually congenial to me. The bullfrogs trump to usher in the night, and the note of the whip-poor-will is borne on the rippling wind from over the water. Sympathy with the fluttering alder and poplar leaves almost takes away my breath; yet, like the lake, my serenity is rippled but not ruffled. These small waves raised by the evening wind are as remote from storm as the smooth reflecting surface. Though it is now dark, the mind still blows and roars in the wood, the waves still dash, and some creatures lull the rest with their notes. The repose is never complete. The wildest animals do not repose, but seek their prey now; the fox, and skunk, and rabbit, now roam the fields and woods without fear. They are Nature's watchmen—links which connect the days of animated life.

When I return to my house I find that visitors have been there and left their cards, either a bunch of flowers, or a wreath of evergreen, or a name in pencil on a yellow walnut leaf or a chip. They who come rarely to the woods take some little piece of the forest into their hands to play with by the way, which they leave, either intentionally or accidentally. One has peeled a willow wand, woven it into a ring, and dropped it on my table. I could always tell if visitors had called in my absence, either by the bended twigs or grass, or the print of their shoes, and generally of what sex or age or quality they were by some slight trace left, as a flower dropped, or a bunch of grass plucked and thrown away, even as far off as the railroad, half a mile distant, or by the lingering odor of a cigar or pipe. Nay, I was frequently notified of the passage of a traveler along the highway sixty rods off by the scent of his pipe.

There is commonly sufficient space about us. Our horizon is never quite at our elbows. The thick wood is not just at our door, nor the pond, but somewhat is always clearing, familiar and worn by us, appropriated and fenced in some way, and reclaimed from Nature. For what reason have I this vast range and circuit, some square miles of unfrequented forest, for my privacy, abandoned to me by men? My nearest neighbor is a mile distant, and no house is visible from any place but the hill-tops within half a mile of my own. I have my horizon bounded by woods all to myself; a distant view of the railroad where it touches the pond on the one hand, and of the fence which skirts the woodland road on the other. But for the most part it is as solitary where I live as on the prairies. It is as much Asia or Africa as New England. I have, as it were, my own sun and moon and stars, and a little world all to myself. At night there was never a traveler passed my house, or knocked at my door, more than if I were the first or last man; unless it were in the spring, when at long intervals some came from the village to fish for pouts—they plainly fished much more in the Walden Pond of their own natures, and baited their hooks with darkness—but they soon retreated, usually with light baskets, and left "the world to darkness and to me," and the black kernel of the night was never profaned by any human neighborhood. I believe that men are generally still a little afraid of the dark, though the witches are all hung, and Christianity and candles have been introduced.

Yet I experienced sometimes that the most sweet and tender, the most innocent and encouraging society may be found in any natural object, even for the poor misanthrope and most melancholy man. There can be no very black melancholy to him who lives in the midst of nature and has his senses still. There was never yet such a storm but it was Aeolian music to a healthy and innocent ear. Nothing can rightly compel a simple and brave man to a vulgar sadness. While I enjoy the friendship of the seasons I trust that nothing can make life a burden to me. The gentle rain which waters my beans and keeps me in the house today is not drear and melancholy, but good for me too. Though it prevents my hoeing them, it is of far more worth than my hoeing. If it should continue so long as to cause the seeds to rot in the ground and destroy the potatoes in the low lands, it would still be good for the grass on the uplands, and, being good for the grass, it would be good for me. Sometimes, when I compare myself with other men, it seems as if I were more favored by the gods than they, beyond any deserts that I am conscious of; as if I had a warrant and surety at their hands which my fellows have not, and were especially guided and guarded. I do not flatter myself, but if it be possible they flatter me. I have never felt lonesome, or in the least oppressed by a sense of solitude, but once, and that was a few weeks after I came to the woods, when, for an hour, I doubted if the near neighborhood of man was not essential to a serene and healthy life. To be alone was something unpleasant. But I was at the same time conscious of a slight insanity in my mood, and seemed to foresee my recovery. In the midst of a gentle rain while these thoughts prevailed, I was suddenly sensible of such sweet and beneficent society in Nature, in the very pattering of the drops, and in every sound and sight around my house, an infinite and unaccountable friendliness all at once like an atmosphere sustaining me, as made the fancied advantages of human neighborhood insignificant, and I have never thought of them since. Every little pine needle expanded and swelled with sympathy and befriended me. I was so distinctly made aware of the presence of something kindred to me, even in scenes which we are accustomed to call wild and dreary, and also that the nearest of blood to me and humanest was not a person nor a villager, that I thought no place could ever be strange to me again.

> Mourning untimely consumes the sad;
> Few are their days in the land of the living,
> Beautiful daughter of Toscar

Some of my pleasantest hours were during the long rain-storms in the spring or fall, which confined me to the house for the afternoon as well as the forenoon, soothed by their ceaseless roar and pelting; when an early twilight ushered in a long evening in which many thoughts had time to take root and unfold themselves. In those driving northeast rains which tried the village houses so, when the maids stood ready with mop and pail in front entries to keep the deluge out, I sat behind my door in my little house, which was all entry, and thoroughly enjoyed its protection. In one heavy thunder-shower the lightning struck a large pitch pine across the pond, making a very conspicuous and perfectly regular spiral groove from top to bottom, an inch or more deep, and four or five inches wide, as you would groove a walking-stick. I passed it again the other day, and was struck with awe on looking up and beholding that mark, now more distinct than ever, where a terrific and resistless bolt came down out of the harmless sky eight years ago. Men frequently say to me, "I should think you would feel lonesome down there, and want to be nearer to folks, rainy and snowy days and nights especially." I am tempted to reply to such—This whole earth which we inhabit is but a point in space. How far apart, think you, dwell the two most distant inhabitants of yonder star, the breadth of whose disk cannot be appreciated by our instruments? Why should I feel lonely? is not our planet in the Milky Way? This which you put seems to me not to be the most important question. What sort of space is that which separates a man from his fellows and makes him solitary? I have found that no exertion of the legs can bring two minds much nearer to one another. What do we want most to dwell near to? Not to many men surely, the depot, the post office, the barroom, the meetinghouse, the schoolhouse, the grocery, Beacon Hill, or the Five Points, where men most congregate, but to the perennial source of our life, whence in all our experience we have found that to issue, as the willow stands near the water and sends out its roots in that direction. This will vary with different natures, but this is the place where a wise man will dig his cellar . . . I one evening overtook one of my townsmen, who has accumulated what is called "a handsome property"—though I never got a *fair* view of it—on the Walden road, driving a pair of cattle to market, who inquired of me how I could bring my mind to give up so many of the comforts of life. I answered that I was very sure I liked it passably well; I was not joking. And so I went home to my bed, and left him to pick his way through the darkness and the mud to Brighton—or Brighttown—which place he would reach some time in the morning.

Any prospect of awakening or coming to life to a dead man makes indifferent all times and places. The place where that may occur is always the same, and indescribably pleasant to all our senses. For the most part we allow only outlying and transient circumstances to make our occasions. They are, in fact, the cause of our distraction. Nearest to all things is that power which fashions their being. *Next* to us the grandest laws are continually being executed. *Next* to us is not the workman whom we have hired, with whom we love so well to talk, but the workman whose work we are.

"How vast and profound is the influence of the subtile powers of Heaven and of Earth!"

"We seek to perceive them, and we do not see them; we seek to hear them, and we do not hear them; identified with the substance of things, they cannot be separated from them."

"They cause that in all the universe men purify and sanctify their hearts, and clothe themselves in their holiday garments to offer sacrifices and oblations to their ancestors. It is an ocean of subtle intelligences. They are everywhere, above us, on our left, on our right; they environ us on all sides."

We are the subjects of an experiment which is not a little interesting to me. Can we not do without the society of our gossips a little while under these circumstances—have our own thoughts to cheer us? Confucius says truly, "Virtue does not remain as an abandoned orphan; it must of necessity have neighbors."

With thinking we may be beside ourselves in a sane sense. By a conscious effort of the mind we can stand aloof from actions and their consequences; and all things, good and bad, go by us like a torrent. We are not wholly involved in Nature. I may be either the driftwood in the stream, or Indra in the sky looking down on it. I may be affected by a theatrical exhibition; on the other hand, I *may not* be affected by an actual event which appears to concern me much more. I only know myself as a human entity; the scene, so to speak, of thoughts and affections; and am sensible of a certain doubleness by which I can stand as remote from myself as from another. However intense my experience, I am conscious of the presence and criticism of a part of me, which, as it were, is not a part of me, but spectator, sharing no experience, but taking note of it, and that is no more I than it is you. When the play, it may be the tragedy, of life is over, the spectator goes his way. It was a kind of fiction, a work of the imagination only, so far as he was concerned. This doubleness may easily make us poor neighbors and friends sometimes.

I find it wholesome to be alone the greater part of the time. To be in company, even with the best, is soon wearisome and dissipating. I love to be alone. I never found the companion that was so companionable as solitude. We are for the most part more lonely when we go abroad among men than when we stay in our chambers. A man thinking or working is always alone, let him be where he will. Solitude is not measured by the miles of space that intervene between a man and his fellows. The really diligent student in one of the crowded hives of Cambridge College is as solitary as a dervis in the desert. The farmer can work alone in the field or the woods all day, hoeing or chopping, and not feel lonesome, because he is employed; but when he comes home at night he cannot sit down in a room alone, at the mercy of his thoughts, but must be where he can "see the folks," and recreate, and, as he thinks, remunerate himself for his day's solitude; and hence he wonders how the student can sit alone in the house all night and most of the day without ennui and "the blues"; but he does not realize that the student, though in the house, is still at work in *his* field, and chopping in *his* woods, as the farmer in his, and in turn seeks the same recreation and society that the latter does, though it may be a more condensed form of it.

Society is commonly too cheap. We meet at very short intervals, not having had time to acquire any new value for each other. We meet at meals three times a day, and give each other a new taste of that old musty cheese that we are. We have had to agree on a certain set of rules, called etiquette and politeness, to make this frequent meeting tolerable and that we need not come to open war. We meet at the post office, and at the sociable, and about the fireside every night; we live thick and are in each other's way, and stumble over one another, and I think that we thus lose some respect for one another. Certainly less frequency would suffice for all important and hearty communications. Consider the girls in a factory—never alone, hardly in their dreams. It would be better if there were but one inhabitant to a square mile, as where I live. The value of a man is not in his skin, that we should touch him.

I have heard of a man lost in the woods and dying of famine and exhaustion at the foot of a tree, whose loneliness was relieved by the grotesque visions with which, owing to bodily weakness, his diseased imagination surrounded him, and which he believed to be real. So also, owing to bodily and mental health and strength, we may be continually cheered by a like but more normal and natural society, and come to know that we are never alone.

I have a great deal of company in my house; especially in the morning, when nobody calls. Let me suggest a few comparisons, that some one may convey an idea of my situation. I am no more lonely than the loon in the pond that laughs so loud, or than Walden Pond itself. What company has that lonely lake, I pray? And yet it has not the blue devils, but the blue angels in it, in the azure tint of its waters. The sun is alone, except in thick weather, when there sometimes appear to be two, but one is a mock sun. God is alone—but the devil, he is far from being alone; he sees a great deal of company; he is legion. I am no more lonely than a single mullein or dandelion in a pasture, or a bean leaf, or sorrel, or a horse-fly, or a bumblebee. I am no more lonely than the Mill Brook, or a weathercock, or the north star, or the south wind, or an April shower, or a January thaw, or the first spider in a new house.

I have occasional visits in the long winter evenings, when the snow falls fast and the wind howls in the wood, from an old settler and original proprietor, who is reported to have dug Walden Pond, and stoned it, and fringed it with pine woods; who tells me stories of old time and of new eternity; and between us we manage to pass a cheerful evening with social mirth and pleasant views of things, even without apples or cider—a most wise and humorous friend, whom I love much, who keeps himself more secret than ever did Goffe or Whalley; and though he is thought to be dead, none can show where he is buried. An elderly dame, too, dwells in my neighborhood, invisible to most persons, in whose odorous herb garden I love to stroll sometimes, gathering simples and listening to her fables; for she has a genius of unequalled fertility, and her memory runs back farther than mythology, and she can tell me the original of every fable, and on what fact every one is founded, for the incidents occurred when she was young. A ruddy and lusty old dame, who delights in all weathers and seasons, and is likely to outlive all her children yet.

The indescribable innocence and beneficence of Nature—of sun and wind and rain, of summer and winter—such health, such cheer, they afford forever! and such sympathy have they ever with our race, that all Nature would be affected, and the sun's brightness fade, and the winds would sigh humanely, and the clouds rain tears, and the woods shed their leaves and put on mourning in midsummer, if any man should ever for a just cause grieve. Shall I not have intelligence with the earth? Am I not partly leaves and vegetable mould myself?

What is the pill which will keep us well, serene, contented? Not my or thy great-grandfather's, but our great-grandmother Nature's universal, vegetable, botanic medicines, by which she has kept herself young always, outlived so many old Parrs in her day, and fed her health with their decaying fatness. For my panacea, instead of one of those quack vials of a mixture dipped from Acheron and the Dead Sea, which come out of those long shallow black-schooner looking wagons which we sometimes see made to carry bottles, let me have a draught of undiluted morning air. Morning air! If men will not drink of this at the fountainhead of the day, why, then, we must even bottle up some and sell it in the shops, for the benefit of those who have lost their subscription ticket to morning time in this world. But remember, it will not keep quite till noonday even in the coolest cellar, but drive out the stopples long ere that and follow westward the steps of Aurora. I am no worshipper of Hygeia, who was the daughter of that old herb-doctor Esculapius, and who is represented on monuments holding a serpent in one hand, and in the other a cup out of which the serpent sometimes drinks; but rather of Hebe, cupbearer to Jupiter, who was the daughter of Juno and wild lettuce, and who had the power of restoring gods and men to the vigor of youth. She was probably the only thoroughly sound-conditioned, healthy, and robust young lady that ever walked the globe, and wherever she came it was spring.

CONCLUSION

To the sick the doctors wisely recommend a change of air and scenery. Thank Heaven, here is not all the world. The buckeye does not grow in New England, and the mockingbird is rarely heard here. The wild goose is more of a cosmopolite than we; he breaks his fast in Canada, takes a luncheon in the Ohio, and plumes himself for the night in a southern bayou. Even the bison, to some extent, keeps pace with the seasons cropping the pastures of the Colorado only till a greener and sweeter grass awaits him by the Yellowstone. Yet we think that if rail fences are pulled down, and stone walls piled up on our farms, bounds are henceforth set to our lives and our fates decided. If you are chosen town clerk, forsooth, you cannot go to Tierra del Fuego this summer: but you may go to the land of infernal fire nevertheless. The universe is wider than our views of it.

Yet we should oftener look over the tafferel of our craft, like curious passengers, and not make the voyage like stupid sailors picking oakum. The other side of the globe is but the home of our correspondent. Our voyaging is only great-circle sailing, and the doctors prescribe for diseases of the skin merely. One hastens to southern Africa to chase the giraffe; but surely that is not the game he would be after. How long, pray, would a man hunt giraffes if he could? Snipes and woodcocks also may afford rare sport; but I trust it would be nobler game to shoot one's self.—

Direct your eye right inward, and you'll find
A thousand regions in your mind
Yet undiscovered. Travel them, and be
Expert in home-cosmography.

What does Africa—what does the West stand for? Is not our own interior white on the chart? black though it may prove, like the coast, when discovered. Is it the source of the Nile, or the Niger, or the Mississippi, or a Northwest Passage around this continent, that we would find? Are these the problems which most concern mankind? Is Franklin the only man who is lost, that his wife should be so earnest to find him? Does Mr. Grinnell know where he himself is? Be rather the Mungo Park, the Lewis and Clark and Frobisher, of your own streams and oceans; explore your own higher latitudes—with shiploads of preserved meats to support you, if they be necessary; and pile the empty cans sky-high for a sign. Were preserved meats invented to preserve meat merely? Nay, be a Columbus to whole new continents and worlds within you, opening new channels, not of trade, but of thought. Every man is the lord of a realm beside which the earthly empire of the Czar is but a petty state, a hummock left by the ice. Yet some can be patriotic who have no *self*-respect, and sacrifice the greater to the less. They love the soil which makes their graves, but have no sympathy with the spirit which may still animate their clay. Patriotism is a maggot in their heads. What was the meaning of that South-Sea Exploring Expedition, with all its parade and expense, but an indirect recognition of the fact that there are continents and seas in the moral world to which every man is an isthmus or an inlet, yet unexplored by him, but that it is easier to sail many thousand miles through cold and storm and cannibals, in a government ship, with five hundred men and boys to assist one, than it is to explore the private sea, the Atlantic and Pacific Ocean of one's being alone.—

> Erret, et extremos alter scrutetur Iberos.
> Plus habet hic vitae, plus habet ille viae.

> Let them wander and scrutinize the outlandish
> Australians.

I have more of God, they more of the road.

It is not worth the while to go round the world to count the cats in Zanzibar. Yet do this even till you can do better, and you may perhaps find some "Symmes' Hole" by which to get at the inside at last. England and France, Spain and Portugal, Gold Coast and Slave Coast, all front on this private sea; but no bark from them has ventured out of sight of land, though it is without doubt the direct way to India. If you would learn to speak all tongues and conform to the customs of all nations, if you would travel farther than all travelers, be naturalized in all climes, and cause the Sphinx to dash her head against a stone, even obey the precept of the old philosopher, and Explore thyself. Herein are demanded the eye and the nerve. Only the defeated and deserters go to the wars, cowards that run away and enlist. Start now on that farthest western way, which does not pause at the Mississippi or the

Pacific, nor conduct toward a wornout China or Japan, but leads on direct, a tangent to this sphere, summer and winter, day and night, sun down, moon down, and at last earth down too.

It is said that Mirabeau took to highway robbery "to ascertain what degree of resolution was necessary in order to place one's self in formal opposition to the most sacred laws of society." He declared that "a soldier who fights in the ranks does not require half so much courage as a footpad"—"that honor and religion have never stood in the way of a well-considered and a firm resolve." This was manly, as the world goes; and yet it was idle, if not desperate. A saner man would have found himself often enough "in formal opposition" to what are deemed "the most sacred laws of society," through obedience to yet more sacred laws, and so have tested his resolution without going out of his way. It is not for a man to put himself in such an attitude to society, but to maintain himself in whatever attitude he find himself through obedience to the laws of his being, which will never be one of opposition to a just government, if he should chance to meet with such.

I left the woods for as good a reason as I went there. Perhaps it seemed to me that I had several more lives to live, and could not spare any more time for that one. It is remarkable how easily and insensibly we fall into a particular route, and make a beaten track for ourselves. I had not lived there a week before my feet wore a path from my door to the pond-side; and though it is five or six years since I trod it, it is still quite distinct. It is true, I fear, that others may have fallen into it, and so helped to keep it open. The surface of the earth is soft and impressible by the feet of men; and so with the paths which the mind travels. How worn and dusty, then, must be the highways of the world, how deep the ruts of tradition and conformity! I did not wish to take a cabin passage, but rather to go before the mast and on the deck of the world, for there I could best see the moonlight amid the mountains. I do not wish to go below now.

I learned this, at least, by my experiment: that if one advances confidently in the direction of his dreams, and endeavors to live the life which he has imagined, he will meet with a success unexpected in common hours. He will put some things behind, will pass an invisible boundary; new, universal, and more liberal laws will begin to establish themselves around and within him; or the old laws be expanded, and interpreted in his favor in a more liberal sense, and he will live with the license of a higher order of beings. In proportion as he simplifies his life, the laws of the universe will appear less complex, and solitude will not be solitude, nor poverty poverty, nor weakness weakness. If you have built castles in the air, your work need not be lost; that is where they should be. Now put the foundations under them.

It is a ridiculous demand which England and America make, that you shall speak so that they can understand you. Neither men nor toadstools grow so. As if that were important, and there were not enough to understand you without them. As if Nature could support but one order of understandings, could not sustain birds as well as quadrupeds, flying as well as creeping things, and *hush* and *whoa*, which Bright can understand, were the best English. As if there were safety in stupidity alone. I fear chiefly lest my expression may not be *extra-vagant* enough, may not wander far enough beyond the narrow limits of my daily experience, so as to be adequate to the truth of which I have been convinced. *Extra vagance*! it depends on how you are yarded. The migrating buffalo, which seeks new pastures in another latitude, is not extravagant like the cow which kicks over the pail, leaps the cowyard fence, and runs after her calf, in milking time. I desire to speak somewhere *without* bounds; like a man in a waking moment, to men in their waking moments; for I am convinced that I cannot exaggerate enough even to lay the foundation of a true expression. Who that has heard a strain of music feared then lest he should speak extravagantly any more forever? In view of the future or possible, we should live quite laxly and undefined in front, our outlines dim and misty on that side; as our shadows reveal an insensible perspiration toward the sun. The volatile truth of our words should continually betray the inadequacy of the residual statement. Their truth is instantly *translated*; its literal monument alone remains. The words which express our faith and piety are not definite; yet they are significant and fragrant like frankincense to superior natures.

Why level downward to our dullest perception always, and praise that as common sense? The commonest sense is the sense of men asleep, which they express by snoring. Sometimes we are inclined to class those who are once-and-a-half-witted with the half-witted, because we appreciate only a third part of their wit. Some would find fault with the morning red, if they ever got up early enough. "They pretend," as I hear, "that the verses of Kabir have four different senses; illusion, spirit, intellect, and the exoteric doctrine of the Vedas"; but in this part of the world it is considered a ground for complaint if a man's writings admit of more than one interpretation. While England endeavors to cure the potato-rot, will not any endeavor to cure the brain-rot, which prevails so much more widely and fatally?

I do not suppose that I have attained to obscurity, but I should be proud if no more fatal fault were found with my pages on this score than was found with the Walden ice. Southern customers objected to its blue color, which is the evidence of its purity, as if it were muddy, and preferred the Cambridge ice, which is white, but tastes of weeds. The purity men love is like the mists which envelop the earth, and not like the azure ether beyond.

Some are dinning in our ears that we Americans, and moderns generally, are intellectual dwarfs compared with the ancients, or even the Elizabethan men. But what is that to the purpose? A living dog is better than a dead lion. Shall a man go and hang himself because he belongs to the race of pygmies, and not be the biggest pygmy that he can? Let every one mind his own business, and endeavor to be what he was made.

Why should we be in such desperate haste to succeed and in such desperate enterprises? If a man does not keep pace with his companions, perhaps it is because he hears a different drummer. Let him step to the music which he hears, however measured or far away. It is not important that he should mature as soon as an apple tree or an oak. Shall he turn his spring into summer? If the condition of things which we were made for is not yet, what were any reality which we can substitute? We will not be shipwrecked on a vain reality. Shall we with pains erect a heaven of blue glass over ourselves, though when it is done we shall be sure to gaze still at the true ethereal heaven far above, as if the former were not?

There was an artist in the city of Kouroo who was disposed to strive after perfection. One day it came into his mind to make a staff. Having considered that in an imperfect work time is an ingredient, but into a perfect work time does not enter, he said to himself, It shall be perfect in all respects, though I should do nothing else in my life. He proceeded instantly to the forest for wood, being resolved that it should not be made of unsuitable material; and as he searched for and rejected stick after stick, his friends gradually deserted him, for they grew old in their works and died, but he grew not older by a moment. His singleness of purpose and resolution, and his elevated piety, endowed him, without his knowledge, with perennial youth. As he made no compromise with Time, Time kept out of his way, and only sighed at a distance because he could not overcome him. Before he had found a stock in all respects suitable the city of Kouroo was a hoary ruin, and he sat on one of its mounds to peel the stick. Before he had given it the proper shape the dynasty of the Candahars was at an end, and with the point of the stick he wrote the name of the last of that race in the sand, and then resumed his work. By the time he had smoothed and polished the staff Kalpa was no longer the pole-star; and ere he had put on the ferule and the head adorned with precious stones, Brahma had awoke and slumbered many times. But why do I stay to mention these things? When the finishing stroke was put to his work, it suddenly expanded before the eyes of the astonished artist into the fairest of all the creations of Brahma. He had made a new system in making a staff, a world with full and fair proportions; in which, though the old cities and dynasties had passed away, fairer and more glorious ones had taken their places. And now he saw by the heap of shavings still fresh at his feet, that, for him and his work, the former lapse of time had been an illusion, and that no more time had elapsed than is required for a single scintillation from the brain of Brahma to fall on and inflame the tinder of a mortal brain. The material was pure, and his art was pure; how could the result be other than wonderful?

No face which we can give to a matter will stead us so well at last as the truth. This alone wears well. For the most part, we are not where we are, but in a false position. Through an infinity of our natures, we suppose a case, and put ourselves into it, and hence are in two cases at the same time, and it is doubly difficult to get out. In sane moments we regard only the facts, the case that is. Say what you have to say, not what you ought. Any truth is better than make-believe. Tom Hyde, the tinker, standing on the gallows, was asked if he had anything to say. "Tell the tailors," said he, "to remember to make a knot in their thread before they take the first stitch." His companion's prayer is forgotten.

However mean your life is, meet it and live it; do not shun it and call it hard names. It is not so bad as you are. It looks poorest when you are richest. The fault-finder will find faults even in paradise. Love your life, poor as it is. You may perhaps have some pleasant, thrilling, glorious hours, even in a poorhouse. The setting sun is reflected from the windows of the almshouse as brightly as from the rich man's abode; the snow melts before its door as early in the spring. I do not see but a quiet mind may live as contentedly there, and have as cheering thoughts, as in a palace. The town's poor seem to me often to live the most independent lives of any. Maybe they are simply great enough to receive without misgiving. Most think that they are above being supported by the town; but it oftener happens that they are not above supporting themselves by dishonest means, which should be more disreputable. Cultivate poverty like a garden herb, like sage. Do not trouble yourself much to get new things, whether clothes or friends. Turn the old; return to them. Things do not change; we change. Sell your clothes and keep your thoughts. God will see that you do not want society. If I were confined to a corner of a garret all my days, like a spider, the world would be just as large to me while I had my thoughts about me. The philosopher said: "From an army of three divisions one can take away its general, and put it in disorder; from the man the most abject and vulgar one cannot take away his thought." Do not seek so anxiously to be developed, to subject yourself to many influences to be played on; it is all dissipation. Humility like darkness reveals the heavenly lights. The shadows of poverty and meanness gather around us, "and lo! creation widens to our view." We are often reminded that if there were bestowed on us the wealth of Croesus, our aims must still be the same, and our means essentially the same. Moreover, if you are restricted in your range by poverty, if you cannot buy books and newspapers, for instance, you are but confined to the most significant and vital experiences; you are compelled to deal with the material which yields the most sugar and the most starch. It is life near the bone where it is sweetest. You are defended from being a trifler. No man loses ever on a lower level by magnanimity on a higher. Superfluous wealth can buy superfluities only. Money is not required to buy one necessary of the soul.

I live in the angle of a leaden wall, into whose composition was poured a little alloy of bell-metal. Often, in the repose of my mid-day, there reaches my ears a confused *tintinnabulum* from without. It is the noise of my contemporaries. My neighbors tell me of their adventures with famous gentlemen and ladies, what notabilities they met at the dinner-table; but I am no more interested in such things than in the contents of the *Daily Times*. The interest and the conversation are about costume and manners chiefly; but a goose is a goose still, dress it as you will. They tell me of California and Texas, of England and the Indies, of the Hon. Mr. ——— of Georgia or of Massachusetts, all transient and fleeting phenomena, till I am ready to leap from their court-yard like the Mameluke bey. I delight to come to my bearings—not walk in procession with pomp and parade, in a conspicuous place, but to walk even with the Builder of the universe, if I may—not to live in this restless, nervous, bustling, trivial Nineteenth Century, but stand or sit thoughtfully while it goes by. What are men celebrating? They are all on a committee of arrangements, and hourly expect a speech from somebody. God is only the president of the day, and Webster is his orator. I love to weigh, to settle, to gravitate toward that which most strongly and rightfully attracts me—not hang by the beam of the scale and try to weigh less—not suppose a case, but take the case that is; to travel the only path I can, and that on which no power can resist me. It affords me no satisfaction to commerce to spring an arch before I have got a solid foundation. Let us not play at kittlybenders. There is a solid bottom everywhere. We read that the traveller asked the boy if the swamp before him had a hard bottom. The boy replied that it had. But presently the traveller's horse sank in up to the girths, and he observed to the boy, "I thought you said that this bog had a hard bottom." "So it has," answered the latter, "but you have not got half way to it yet." So it is with the bogs and quicksands of society; but he is an old boy that knows it. Only what is thought, said, or done at a certain rare coincidence is good. I would not be one of those who will foolishly drive a nail into mere lath and plastering; such a deed would keep me awake nights. Give me a hammer, and let me feel for the furring. Do not depend on the putty. Drive a nail home and clinch it so faithfully that you can wake up in the night and think of your work with satisfaction — a work at which you would not be ashamed to invoke the Muse. So will help you God, and so only. Every nail driven should be as another rivet in the machine of the universe, you carrying on the work.

Rather than love, than money, than fame, give me truth. I sat at a table where were rich food and wine in abundance, and obsequious attendance, but sincerity and truth were not; and I went away hungry from the inhospitable board. The hospitality was as cold as the ices. I thought that there was no need of ice to freeze them. They talked to me of the age of the wine and the fame of the vintage; but I thought of an older, a newer, and purer wine, of a more glorious vintage, which they had not got, and could not buy. The style, the house and grounds and "entertainment" pass for nothing with me. I called on the king, but he made me wait in his hall, and conducted like a man incapacitated for hospitality. There was a man in my neighborhood who lived in a hollow tree. His manners were truly regal. I should have done better had I called on him.

How long shall we sit in our porticoes practising idle and musty virtues, which any work would make impertinent? As if one were to begin the day with longsuffering, and hire a man to hoe his potatoes; and in the afternoon go forth to practise Christian meekness and charity with goodness aforethought! Consider the China pride and stagnant self-complacency of mankind. This generation inclines a little to congratulate itself on being the last of an illustrious line; and in Boston and London and Paris and Rome, thinking of its long descent, it speaks of its progress in art and science and literature with satisfaction. There are the Records of the Philosophical Societies, and the public Eulogies of *Great Men*! It is the good Adam contemplating his own virtue. "Yes, we have done great deeds, and sung divine songs, which shall never die"—that is, as long as *we* can remember them. The learned societies and great men of Assyria—where are they? What youthful philosophers and experimentalists we are! There is not one of my readers who has yet lived a whole human life. These may be but the spring months in the life of the race. If we have had the seven-years' itch, we have not seen the seventeen-year locust yet in Concord. We are acquainted with a mere pellicle of the globe on which we live. Most have not delved six feet beneath the surface, nor leaped as many above it. We know not where we are. Beside, we are sound asleep nearly half our time. Yet we esteem ourselves wise, and have an established order on the surface. Truly, we are deep thinkers, we are ambitious spirits! As I stand over the insect crawling amid the pine needles on the forest floor, and endeavoring to conceal itself from my sight, and ask myself why it will cherish those humble thoughts, and hide its head from me who might, perhaps, be its benefactor, and impart to its race some cheering information, I am reminded of the greater Benefactor and Intelligence that stands over me the human insect. There is an incessant influx of novelty into the world, and yet we tolerate incredible dulness. I need only suggest what kind of sermons are still listened to in the most enlightened countries. There are such words as joy and sorrow, but they are only the burden of a psalm, sung with a nasal twang, while we believe in the ordinary and mean. We think that we can change our clothes only. It is said that the British Empire is very large and respectable, and that the United States are a first-rate power. We do not believe that a tide rises and falls behind every man which can float the British Empire like a chip, if he should ever harbor it in his mind. Who knows what sort of seventeen-year locust will next come out of the ground? The government of the world I live in was not framed, like that of Britain, in after-dinner conversations over the wine.

The life in us is like the water in the river. It may rise this year higher than man has ever known it, and flood the parched uplands; even this may be the eventful year, which will drown out all our muskrats. It was not always dry land where we dwell. I see far inland the banks which the stream anciently washed, before science began to record its freshets. Every one has heard the story which has gone the rounds of New England, of a strong and beautiful bug which came out of the dry leaf of an old table of apple-tree wood, which had stood in a farmer's kitchen for sixty years, first in Connecticut, and afterward in Massachusetts—from an egg deposited in the living tree many years earlier still, as appeared by counting the annual layers beyond it; which was heard gnawing out for several weeks, hatched perchance by the heat of an urn. Who does not feel his faith in a resurrection and immortality strengthened by hearing of this? Who knows what beautiful and winged life, whose egg has been buried for ages under many concentric layers of woodenness in the dead dry life of society, deposited at first in the alburnum of the green and living tree, which has been gradually converted into the semblance of its well-seasoned tomb—heard perchance gnawing out now for years by the astonished family of man, as they sat round the festive board—may unexpectedly come forth from amidst society's most trivial and handselled furniture, to enjoy its perfect summer life at last!

I do not say that John or Jonathan will realize all this; but such is the character of that morrow which mere lapse of time can never make to dawn. The light which puts out our eyes is darkness to us. Only that day dawns to which we are awake. There is more day to dawn. The sun is but a morning star.

Notes

1. Biographical details have been drawn from Walter Harding, *The Days of Henry Thoreau* (New York: Knopf, 1965); Robert D. Richardson Jr., *Henry David Thoreau: A Life of the Mind* (Berkeley: University of California Press, 1988); Alan Hodder, *Thoreau's Ecstatic Witness* (New Haven: Yale University Press, 2001); William J. Wolf, *Thoreau: Mystic, Prophet, Ecologist* (Philadelphia: United Church Press, 1974); *Letters to a Spiritual Seeker, Henry David Thoreau*, ed. P. Dean Bradley (New York: W. W. Norton, 2004); *The Correspondence of Henry David Thoreau,* ed. Walter Harding and Carl Bode (New York: New York University Press, 1958).

2. Hodder, in *Thoreau's Ecstatic Witness*, 293, suggests that Thoreau's featureless experiences are reminiscent of the apophatic theology of the Western mystical tradition; William J. Wolf, in *Thoreau: Mystic, Prophet, Ecologist*, places Thoreau's experiences within the classical Christian mystical system described by Evelyn Underhill. Walter Harding compares Thoreau's ecstasies to those of Wordsworth.

3. See Hodder, *Thoreau's Ecstatic Witness,* 5–6.

4. Some speculate that Thoreau had a romantic interest in Lydian Emerson based on a letter he wrote her from Staten Island on June 20, 1843. See COR,119–20.

5. An "Oriental Renaissance" began in Europe during the last quarter of the eighteenth century initiated by translations of Hindu texts by the Asiatic Society of Bengal, which produced capable translations of major Indian texts by English scholars residing in India. The texts that most influenced Thoreau were Charles Wilkins's *Bhagavad Gita* (1785) and *Hitopadesa* (1787), William Jones' translation of *The Laws of Manu* (1794), Henry Thomas Colebrooke's translations of the *Samkhya Karikas* (1837), and Horace Hayman Wilson's translation of the *Vishnu Purana* (1840). See Alan D. Hodder, "'Ex Oriente Lux': Thoreau's Ecstasies and the Hindu Texts," *Harvard Theological Review* 66, no. 4 (1993): 403–38.

6. The much-repeated story of Emerson asking Thoreau why he was in jail, only to have Thoreau ask him why he was *not* in jail appears to be apocryphal.

7. See Hodder, *Thoreau's Ecstatic Witness,* 33ff.

8. Thoreau's sexuality has been the subject of scholarly debate, but no consensus has emerged. Walter Harding, a leading Thoreau scholar, concluded that while there were numerous homoerotic references in Thoreau's writings, his sexual orientation is indeterminate. Harding concludes that, in any event, Thoreau had successfully sublimated his sexual energies, whether heterosexual or homosexual, through his worship of nature, and that without this sublimation, Thoreau "might never have become the literary master he did." See Walter Harding, "Thoreau's Sexuality," *Journal of Homosexuality* 21, no. 3 (1991). Online at http://www.kouroo.info/Thoreau/ThoreauAndEros.pdf.

9. See Hodder, *Thoreau's Ecstatic Witness,* 190. Sexual energy (Sanskrit *ojas*, lit. "vigor") is sublimated and finally transmuted through continence and other ascetic disciplines into *tejas* (Sanskrit, lit. "light.").

10. In his introduction to *Walden*, Bill McKibben argues that Thoreau's call for material simplicity remains the central requirement for reversing global warming. WAL, xi–xii.

11. *Walden* was republished in 1866 and has never gone out of print since that time. Although Thoreau died with none of his books in print, by the turn of the century he was regarded among the highest ranks of American literature. His influence on American radical thought and twentieth-century progressive movements has been incalculable, and his influence continues to be felt. Ken Ilgunas's *Walden on Wheels: On the Open Road from Debt to Freedom* (Boston: New Harvest, 2014) chronicles a young graduate student's odyssey to combat student debt using Thoreauvian principles.

12. Harding, *Days of Henry Thoreau*, 466.

13. Thoreau made these remarks while participating in a panel on "The Commercial Spirit of the Modern Times" that was part of his commencement exercises. See Harding, *Days of Henry Thoreau,* 49–50.

14. Thoreau's sexuality remains a matter of academic dispute. See n. 8.

MODERN SPIRITUAL MASTERS

Robert Ellsberg, Series Editor

This series introduces the essential writing and vision of some of the great spiritual teachers of our time. While many of these figures are rooted in long-established traditions of spirituality, others have charted new, untested paths. In each case, however, they have engaged in a spiritual journey shaped by the challenges and concerns of our age. Together with the saints and witnesses of previous centuries, these modern spiritual masters may serve as guides and companions to a new generation of seekers.

Already published:

Modern Spiritual Masters (edited by Robert Ellsberg)

Swami Abhishiktananda (edited by Shirley du Boulay)

Metropolitan Anthony of Sourozh (edited by Gillian Crow)

Eberhard Arnold (edited by Johann Christoph Arnold)

Pedro Arrupe (edited by Kevin F. Burke, S.J.)

Daniel Berrigan (edited by John Dear)

Thomas Berry (edited by Mary EvelynTucker and John Grim)

Dietrich Bonhoeffer (edited by Robert Coles)

Robert McAfee Brown (edited by Paul Crowley)

Dom Helder Camara (edited by Francis McDonagh)

Carlo Carretto (edited by Robert Ellsberg)

G. K. Chesterton (edited by William Griffin)

Joan Chittister (edited by Mary Lou Kownacki and Mary Hembrow Snyder)

Yves Congar (edited by Paul Lakeland)

The Dalai Lama (edited by Thomas A. Forsthoefel)

Alfred Delp, S.J. (introduction by Thomas Merton)

Catherine de Hueck Dogerty (edited by David Meconi, S.J.)

Virgilio Elizondo (edited by Timothy Matovina)

Charles de Foucauld (edited by Robert Ellsberg)

Mohandas Gandhi (edited by John Dear)

Bede Griffiths (edited by Thomas Matus)

Romano Guardini (edited by Robert A. Krieg)

Gustavo Gutiérrez (edited by Daniel G. Groody)

Thich Nhat Hanh (edited by Robert Ellsberg)

Abraham Joshua Heschel (edited by Susannah Heschel)

Etty Hillesum (edited by Annemarie S. Kidder)

Caryll Houselander (edited by Wendy M. Wright)

Pope John XXIII (edited by Jean Maalouf)

Rufus Jones (edited by Kerry Walters)

Clarence Jordan (edited by Joyce Hollyday)

John Main (edited by Laurence Freeman)

Anthony de Mello (edited by William Dych, S.J.)

Thomas Merton (edited by Christine M. Bochen)

John Muir (edited by Tim Flinders)

John Henry Newman (edited by John T. Ford, C.S.C.)

Henri Nouwen (edited by Robert A. Jonas)

Flannery O'Connor (edited by Robert Ellsberg)

Karl Rahner (edited by Philip Endean)

Brother Roger of Taizé (edited by Marcello Fidanzio)

Oscar Romero (by Marie Dennis, Rennie Golden, and Scott Wright)

Albert Schweitzer (edited by James Brabazon)

Frank Sheed and Maisie Ward (edited by David Meconi)

Sadhu Sundar Singh (edited by Charles E. Moore)

Mother Maria Skobtsova (introduction by Jim Forest)

Dorothee Soelle (edited by Dianne L. Oliver)

Edith Stein (edited by John Sullivan, O.C.D.)

David Steindl-Rast (edited by Clare Hallward)

William Stringfellow (edited by Bill Wylie-Kellerman)

Pierre Teilhard de Chardin (edited by Ursula King)

Mother Teresa (edited by Jean Maalouf)

St. Thérèse of Lisieux (edited by Mary Frohlich)

Howard Thurman (edited by Mary Krohlich)

Leo Tolstoy (edited by Charles E. Moore)

Evelyn Underhill (edited by Emilie Griffin)

Jean Vanier (edited by Carolyn Whitney-Brown)

Swami Vivekananda (edited by Victor M. Parachin)

Simone Weil (edited by Eric O. Springsted)

John Howard Yoder (edited by Paul Martens and Jenny Howells)